Joan of Arc

Joan of Arc

Other books in the Heroes and Villains series include:

Alexander the Great
Al Capone
Frederick Douglass
Adolf Hitler
Saddam Hussein
King Arthur
Martin Luther King Jr.
Josef Mengele
Pol Pot
Oskar Schindler

.

Heroes and Villains

Joan of Arc

Elizabeth Silverthorne

LUCENT BOOKS
An imprint of Thomson Gale, a part of The Thomson Corporation

THOMSON
GALE

Detroit • New York • San Francisco • San Diego • New Haven, Conn. • Waterville, Maine • London • Munich

LIBRARY OF CONGRESS CATALOGING-IN-PUBLICATION DATA

Silverthorne, Elizabeth, 1930-
  Joan of Arc / by Elizabeth Silverthorne.
    p. cm. — (Heroes and villains series)
  Includes bibliographical references and index.
  ISBN 1-59018-554-4 (hard cover : alk. paper)
  1. Joan, of Arc, Saint, 1412-1431. 2. Christian saints—France—Biography. 3. France—History—Charles VII, 1422-1461. I. Title. II. Series.
  DC103.S468 2005
  944'.026'092—dc22
                                                    2004014756

Contents

Foreword

Good and evil are an ever-present feature of human history. Their presence is reflected through the ages in tales of great heroism and extraordinary villainy. Such tales provide insight into human nature, whether they involve two people or two thousand, for the essence of heroism and villainy is found in deeds rather than in numbers. It is the deeds that pique our interest and lead us to wonder what prompts a man or woman to perform such acts.

Samuel Johnson, the eminent eighteenth-century English writer, once wrote, "The two great movers of the human mind are the desire for good, and fear of evil." The pairing of desire and fear, possibly two of the strongest human emotions, helps explain the intense fascination people have with all things good and evil—and by extension, heroic and villainous.

People are attracted to the person who reaches into a raging river to pull a child from what could have been a watery grave for both, and to the person who risks his or her own life to shepherd hundreds of desperate black slaves to safety on the Underground Railroad. We wonder what qualities these heroes possess that enable them to act against self-interest, and even their own survival. We also wonder if, under similar circumstances, we would behave as they do.

Evil, on the other hand, horrifies as well as intrigues us. Few people can look upon the drifter who mutilates and kills a neighbor or the dictator who presides over the torture and murder of thousands of his own citizens without feeling a sense of revulsion. And yet, as Joseph Conrad writes, we experience "the fascination of the abomination." How else to explain the overwhelming success of a book such as Truman Capote's *In Cold Blood*, which examines in horrifying detail a vicious and senseless murder that took place in the American heartland in the 1960s? The popularity of murder mysteries and Court TV are also evidence of the human fascination with villainy.

Most people recoil in the face of such evil. Yet most feel a deep-seated curiosity about the kind of person who could commit a terrible act. It is perhaps a reflection of our innermost fears that we wonder whether we could resist or stand up to such behavior in our presence or even if we ourselves possess the capacity to commit such terrible crimes.

The Lucent Books Heroes and Villains series capitalizes on our fascination with the perpetrators of both good and evil by introducing readers to some of history's most revered heroes and hated villains. These include heroes such as Frederick Douglass, who knew firsthand the humiliation of slavery and, at great risk to himself, publicly fought to abolish the institution of slavery in America. It also includes villains such as Adolf Hitler, who is remembered both for the devastation of Europe and for the murder of 6 million Jews and thousands of Gypsies, Slavs, and others whom Hitler deemed unworthy of life.

Each book in the Heroes and Villains series examines the life story of a hero or villain from history. Generous use of primary and secondary source quotations gives readers eyewitness views of the life and times of each individual as well as enlivens the narrative. Notes and annotated bibliographies provide stepping-stones to further research.

A Time of Miracles and Mystery

Joan of Arc lived during the Middle Ages, a time when the church defined life for most people in Europe. From the time they were baptized until they were buried in holy ground, religion was the controlling force in their lives. If they lived their lives according to the will of God—as explained to them by their priests, who in turn took their guidance from the church hierarchy headed by the pope—they hoped that when they died they would spend eternity in God's presence. The alternative was to be condemned to hell.

God, heaven, the devil, and hell were very real to them. Few people could read, but in their churches and cathedrals murals and stained glass windows vividly pictured the glories of heaven and the torments of hell. Devout churchgoers believed these portrayals were accurate. Under the circumstances, the idea that God (or Satan) might talk directly to someone was also completely believable.

Priests also taught that the path to salvation could be smoothed if one contributed money to the church. As a result, the medieval church had enormous wealth. It owned magnificent cathedrals, huge monasteries, great libraries, and vast amounts of land. Many in the church's hierarchy lived in luxury even as they extolled the virtues of a life of poverty and humility.

Besides being enormously wealthy, the church had great political power. Its influence was broad, and even the king was subject to its direction. At their coronations rulers received their legitimacy from the church, and by extension from God, through the ritual of consecration with holy oil. A monarch ignored church doctrine at his or her peril. Even powerful monarchs, if they disobeyed the church, could be excommunicated, denying them access to the sacraments necessary for salvation. And more immediately, excommunication meant a ruler could no longer demand the loyalty of his or her subjects.

During the Middle Ages, the church wielded tremendous political power. In this medieval painting, Pope Leo III himself crowns Charlemagne emperor in 800.

Disobeying the church implied that one was in conflict with church doctrine, and that opened a person to charges of heresy. A heretic was subject to imprisonment, torture, and death—unless one had enough political power to force church officials to back down. Since heresy was considered a crime against the state as well as against the church, convicted heretics were usually turned over to civil authorities for punishment after being convicted.

Supernatural Influences

Closely connected to religious beliefs in Joan of Arc's time were beliefs in supernatural forces, such as witchcraft. Merely to be suspected of witchcraft put an individual in grave peril; bringing a charge of witchcraft against someone was often all it took to destroy him or her politically. Because she represented a threat to their hold on power, Joan's enemies often accused her of being a witch.

War

In addition to religion, war was a fact of life for people in Joan of Arc's time. France in the Middle Ages was not a unified nation. Instead, like most of Europe, France was a patchwork of feudal domains called duchies, which were ruled by powerful dukes. The leaders of these domains strove to broaden their holdings, and war was the frequent consequence. This continual jockeying for power resulted in frequent shifts of allegiance among the residents of disputed territory. In border regions, such as the one where Joan lived, even villages a couple of miles apart could be divided from one another politically.

For the people of France, conflict with England had long been part of their lives. Historians would one day refer to this as the Hundred Years' War, although it was actually a series of wars interrupted by treaties and truces. At the time of Joan's birth the English had won most of the important battles, and three years later the war took a definite turn for the worse for France. Against this background of religious and patriotic passion, and belief in the supernatural, the drama of Joan of Arc's life played out.

Chapter One

LIFE IN DOMREMY

Joan of Arc was twelve years old when she first heard the "voices" that would guide her future actions. Before then she led the life typical of any young peasant girl living in a small village in war-torn France in the early fifteenth century. After the voices spoke to her she became a different person. From that time on her life was dedicated to following the instructions she believed her heavenly advisers were giving her.

The Village

Joan of Arc was born in the small village of Domremy in northeastern France, most likely on or about January 6, 1412, according to the testimony of Joan herself and of other people from her village. Sometime in January of 1412 the new baby was baptized Jhenette (little Joan) in the church of Domremy with ten godmothers and godfathers in attendance. Her parents Isabelle and Jacques already had three sons, Jacques, Pierre, and Jean. Another daughter, Catherine, would be born after Jhenette. Only after she left her native village at the age of sixteen would Jhenette be known as Jehanne (or Joan in English).

The political patchwork that was France in the early fifteenth century caused the region where Joan grew up, in the pleasant valley of the wandering Meuse River, to be a place of frequent turmoil. Part of the valley belonged to France and the other part to the duchy (dukedom) of Lorraine, which was allied to yet another duchy known as Burgundy. The powerful Duke of Burgundy, in turn, was an ally of England's King Henry V, who claimed

In January 1412 Joan of Arc was born in this house in the small village of Domremy in northeastern France.

Joan's Name

Joan, and the people who met her, never heard the name "Joan of Arc." Usually people in fifteenth-century France used given names plus a place name to identify themselves and only occasionally used surnames. She called herself Jehanne la Pucelle (Joan the Maid) because it emphasized the chastity she had sworn to keep as she performed her mission. This is the way she signed the letters she dictated, calling upon the English leaders to surrender to her. After she led the forces that lifted the siege of Orléans, she was often referred to as the "Maid of Orléans." During her lifetime, both her friends and enemies referred to her as "The Maid."

It was not until twenty-four years after her death that the family name was written as "Darc," and it was not until the sixteenth century that the apostrophe was added. A wide variety of spellings of the family name occurred over the years before "d'Arc" became the common designation.

the right to the French throne as well. Domremy's residents considered themselves loyal subjects of the French king, and the children of the village learned early in life to hate the English and their Burgundian allies.

Almost all of the people living in Domremy were farmers. Although most owned a few sheep, cattle, and pigs, everyone was poor and life was difficult. They had to provide for themselves every necessity of life: build their own houses, produce food for themselves and their animals, make their own furniture, clothing, and tools. Everyone worked hard, including children as soon as they were able.

Although the countryside was delightful during the brief summer months, for most of the year it was damp and cold. No matter what the weather, crops and animals had to be taken care of, and children were expected to do their part. Boys and girls helped with planting, weeding, and harvesting crops, and all children took turns driving cows and sheep to pasture and watching over them during the day.

Such an existence left little or no time for school. Although the children of the nobility were taught by tutors, most children (and most adults) did not know how to read or write. Joan learned to count a little, but even after she was grown she could sign her name only if someone who was literate guided her hand.

The Family

Animals and people lived side by side in the forty or fifty houses that made up

This painting shows a pastoral scene in Domremy. Although some villagers owned a few sheep, cattle, or pigs, most were poor and led difficult lives.

the village of Domremy. Like those of their neighbors, the stone cottage in which Joan and her family lived was small and dark with a dirt floor. It had none of the amenities or comforts of modern houses. Joan's family was better off than most, since her father held a position that carried with it some prestige. Jacques was considered responsible, honest, and intelligent by the townspeople, and they elected him sergeant of Domremy, a position ranking third after

the mayor and sheriff. Among his duties were collecting taxes and representing the townspeople in disputes.

Like most of the town's residents, Jacques and Isabelle were hardworking, devout Christians. Isabelle taught her children to say the Apostles' Creed, the Ave Maria, and the Lord's Prayer. She also taught her daughters household tasks and especially the arts of spinning and sewing. At an early age girls learned to spin wool using a distaff, a handheld stick wrapped with wool fiber that was drawn through a notched end and twisted into thread with the fingers. Women commonly carried a distaff with them and would spin whenever they had a few free moments. Joan became an expert spinner; she was also proud of her skill as a seamstress.

From all accounts of Joan's childhood it is clear that hers was typical of most girls of the time. Like all the children in Domremy she took her turn working in the fields and driving the village cattle and sheep to pasture, but she preferred doing housework and especially liked practicing her sewing and spinning skills. Years later, when she was asked if she had learned any trade in her youth, she replied: "Yes, to sew linen cloths and to spin. . . . When I was in my father's house, I busied myself with the housework."[1]

Religion

Although Joan led an ordinary life in most ways, what set her apart was an extreme piety—even though this was a time when virtually everyone attended church. Her friends sometimes teased her because she was so eager to attend Mass and go to confession and spent so much time praying. Joan was also loving and caring and giving toward the poor and the sick. Years after her death many people who had known her as a young girl attested to her religious devotion and to her goodness.

A childhood friend, Mengrette Joyart, testified:

My father's house was almost adjoining Joan's and I knew Joan the Maid, for often I span thread in her company and with her did other house tasks, day and night. She was brought up in the Christian religion and full of good ways, as it seemed. She went of her own will and often to church and gave alms out of her father's property and was so good, simple and pious that I and the other young girls would tell her that she was too pious.[2]

Perrin Drappier, who had been churchwarden in the church at Domremy during Joan's early years, confirmed her devoutness as a child. He said, "When I did not ring the bells for Compline [the last religious service of the day], Joan would catch me and scold me, saying that I had not done well; and she even promised to give me some wool if I would be punctual in ringing for Compline. . . . She gave much in alms; she worked with a will, spinning and doing the necessary tasks."[3]

Pastimes

Though she was devout and hardworking, Joan gladly joined the other children of the village in play. Despite the fact that their daily lives were a constant round of physical tasks connected with plowing, sowing, harvesting,

French Civil War

When Joan the Maid appeared on the scene, France was in deep despair. Not only was it besieged by the English, it was also torn apart by civil strife as John of Burgundy and Bernard of Armagnac and their followers struggled for control of the government. During this struggle, thousands upon thousands of Frenchmen were killed, tortured, maimed, and imprisoned. On one bloody weekend in June 1418 sixteen hundred people were massacred in Paris, including Bernard of Armagnac. For decades underpaid soldiers from both sides terrorized and stripped the country, and even more people died of starvation than in battle. Orléans was under siege by the English invaders in 1428, and if it fell France would also fall. In vain France looked to Charles VII for leadership. A strong military leader, one who could inspire loyalty and unite the country, was desperately needed.

sewing, spinning, baking, gardening, preserving, and caring for the animals, the children enjoyed strenuous games such as tag, leap frog, and foot races. Joan was especially good at racing.

She and her friends also enjoyed the church festivals and holidays around which life in medieval France revolved. The fourth Sunday in Lent, Laetare Sunday, was a favorite church festival day. In those days there was a dense forest near the village, and at the edge of the forest was a huge old beech tree. Some of the old people of the village called it the Fairies' Tree and said that in ancient times the fairies used to come out at night and dance around it. For Joan and her friends, however, it was just a grand old tree with branches that swept down to the ground. According to a long-standing tradition they made garlands of wildflowers to hang on its branches and sang and danced around the tree. It was also where they gathered to picnic on nuts and specially made flat cakes after Mass on Laetare Sunday.

The War

Whatever they were doing—working, playing, or praying—the villagers of Domremy were constantly aware of danger because of the war with England that had started long before most of the people were born. Day and night the men took turns watching from the church tower for signs of attack. When the watcher spied approaching soldiers he would ring the church bells. This was the signal for the villagers to quickly round up their families and livestock and flee to an abandoned castle on an island in the Meuse River. They would remain in this stronghold until the troops, who could be expected to take anything of value, passed on to the next village. The children became used to helping round up the animals and drive them to the refuge at the sound of the alarm.

The war had long been one in which the French had fought the English and their Burgundian allies to a standstill. But this changed in 1415, when a decisive battle took place between the English and French armies near the village of Agincourt in northern France. The battle was an overwhelming victory for the English under

French and English soldiers engage in battle near Agincourt, France, in 1415. Led by King Henry V (left center), English forces soundly defeated the French.

The Voices

The voices and visions that Joan believed were sent from God to help her save France have caused much controversy and resulted in endless theories. George Bernard Shaw called her a "visualizer." In an introduction to his insightful play, Saint Joan, *which is reprinted in Wilfred T. Jewkes and Jerome B. Landfield,* Joan of Arc: Fact, Legend, and Literature, *Shaw explains:*

> Joan's voices and visions have played many tricks with her reputation. They have been held to prove that she was mad, that she was a liar and impostor, that she was a sorceress (she was burned for this), and finally that she was a saint. They do not prove any of these things; but the variety of the conclusions reached shew how little our matter-of-fact historians know about other people's minds, or even about their own. There are people in the world whose imagination is so vivid that when they have an idea it comes to them as an audible voice, sometimes uttered by a visible figure.

Shaw went on to name other famous people in history who have had similar experiences of hearing voices or seeing visions, including Socrates, St. Francis, Martin Luther, and William Blake.

the leadership of their king, Henry V, who went on to conquer all of Normandy. Gradually more and more of France fell to the English. In 1417 Henry V laid siege to the French town of Rouen, and fifty thousand French died of starvation before the city surrendered. In 1419 he advanced on Paris, which had been devastated by an epidemic of the plague the previous year.

The following year the Treaty of Troyes between the English, French, and Burgundians was signed. Queen Isabelle of France conspired with the Duke of Burgundy to have her hus-band sign the treaty that disinherited her own son. The noted historian Will Durant says of this agreement: "France, by the Treaty of Troyes (1420), surrendered everything, even honor. Charles VI gave his daughter Katherine [Catherine] to Henry V in marriage, promised to bequeath to him the French throne, turned over to him the governance of France, and, to clear up any ambiguity, disowned the Dauphin [the heir to the throne] as his son."[4]

Despite the concessions it contained, the Treaty of Troyes did not bring peace to France. In 1422 both

Henry V of England and Charles VI of France died, and the Dauphin (who with his loyalist followers still held southern France) immediately repudiated the treaty and declared that he was Charles VII, king of France. The English did not agree. They declared that the son of Henry V and Catherine, Henry VI, was king of France. Since Henry VI was not yet a year old, the infant's uncle, the Duke of Bedford, was sent to rule France as his regent.

Meanwhile, robber bands of demobilized soldiers (both French and English) roamed freely in France, terrorizing the people. The Duke of Bedford tried to impose order, hanging some ten thousand bandits in a single year, but the violence continued. In Domremy as in other French villages, dread and hatred of the English occupiers and their Burgundian allies grew even stronger as the devastation went on year after year.

The Voices

In the summer of 1424 in Domremy a miraculous event destined to change the course of the war occurred. Joan later recalled that she was alone one day in her father's garden when about noontime she heard someone speaking to her. Joan said that she was "in her thirteenth year"—that is, twelve years old—when this happened. At first she was greatly alarmed, as she later related: "I was in my thirteenth year when God sent a voice to guide me. At first,

I was very much frightened. The voice came towards the hour of noon, in summer, in my father's garden. . . . I heard the voice on my right hand, in the direction of the church. I seldom hear it without seeing a light. That light always appears on the side from which I hear the voice."[5]

The first two times she heard the voice, she did not know who was speaking, but the third time she saw the speaker and it was the archangel Michael, the defender of France. In this vision the archangel was surrounded by many shining angels and spoke to her so kindly and gently that Joan was no longer afraid. He urged her to go often to church and to lead a good and pure life—which Joan had done for as long as she could remember. Then Michael told her that St. Catherine and St. Margaret would appear to her and guide her. She must believe all that they told her and follow their advice, he said, for the messages they gave her would be from God. Joan had often prayed to these two saints, who were said to have been virgins who died for their faith. When they appeared to her in a cloud of light wearing golden crowns and surrounded by a sweet fragrance, she knelt and embraced their feet, promising them that she would remain a virgin for as long as doing so pleased God.

The voices and visions appeared to her often, sometimes three times a week—often when church bells were ringing. For four years she kept them

At the age of twelve, Joan of Arc began to hear the voices of angels that told her she had been chosen to save France from the English.

secret from her family and friends. She was afraid she would not be believed or that she would be thought to be crazy. She may have described them to her priest during confession; whether she did so is uncertain, since a priest is prohibited from revealing what is said during confession. She longed to go with her heavenly visitors, but they told her that God had important work for her to do on earth.

While she waited for the voices to instruct her, she worked and prayed. Then, when she was sixteen, the war intensified. The voices became more urgent and their instructions more explicit. St. Michael, St. Margaret, and St. Catherine appeared and told her that she must leave Domremy and go to aid France's king. When she heard this, Joan was dismayed. She loved King Charles, but she wondered what a poor uneducated country girl like herself could do to help him. The visions reassured her. She had been chosen to save France, they said, and they would guide her. They warned her, however, that she would have only a year in which to carry out the mission assigned to her by God.

Chapter Two

THE MISSION BEGINS

When the voices told Joan that she was the only one who could save France, she set out to do so despite all opposition. She agreed with those who saw her as an improbable savior, but several circumstances helped her win converts to her cause. Everyone in France, from the Dauphin on down, believed the English were about to take over the whole country, and there was a desperate willingness to grasp at any straw of hope. There was, moreover, an old prophecy that said a maiden would save France. Above all, there was Joan's persistent, unshakable faith that she had been chosen by God for this task.

Leaving Domremy

Key to Joan's mission was the strong fortress of Vaucouleurs, located a short distance from Domremy, on the banks of the Meuse River. Its location meant the fortress was in Burgundian territory, but it had remained loyal to the Dauphin. This stubborn pocket of resistance annoyed the English, and in June 1428 the Duke of Bedford decided to besiege Vaucouleurs. Robert de Baudricourt, the captain in command of the fort, refused to surrender. As hordes of soldiers crowded into the valley, destroying crops and looting homes, the peasants in the small villages fled. This time the abandoned castle in the river Meuse was not likely to withstand such a large force. Driving their cattle before them, Joan's family, along with the other inhabitants of Domremy, sought refuge in Neufchateau, the nearest fortified city. Eventually the attackers went on to ransack other villages, and the residents of Domremy returned

The voice of the archangel Michael (pictured in a Byzantine mosaic) instructed Joan to persuade the Dauphin to give her control of the French army.

Joan's Saints

All three of Joan's main apparitions are usually pictured wearing swords. The archangel Michael appears in the Old Testament as one of the four great angels. He is described as a military leader in the war between God and Satan in Revelation 12:7. Frenchmen adopted him as the protective angel of France, and Mont-Saint-Michel in Normandy was the last great fort of French loyalty.

St. Catherine died in 305. After the Roman emperor Maxentius ordered the execution of Christians, Catherine argued so passionately for her faith that the emperor fell in love with her and ordered her to marry him. She refused, saying she would only be the bride of Christ. When the outraged emperor created a machine with wheels to crush her, it was miraculously disabled, so the frustrated executioners beheaded her. St. Margaret, whose statue was in the church of Domremy, was also decapitated for refusing to marry a pagan ruler. Joan would have known the story that she had entered a monastery disguised as a man. In Joan's time pious young girls looked to saints not only as protectors but also as role models.

home to find many of their houses burned and their church in ruins.

During this intensely troubled time, Joan's voices began insisting she go to Chinon, the castle where the Dauphin and his court resided. There, they told her, she must persuade the Dauphin to put her in charge of France's army. Although she protested that she was just a country girl with no military ability, the voices of St. Catherine and St. Margaret persuaded her that God wished her to carry out this mission. Archangel Michael commanded that Joan go to Vaucouleurs and ask for Baudricourt's help in reaching the Dauphin.

Finally Joan was convinced that God not only had assigned her to lead the French forces but that he would give her strength to do his will. However, she first had to get her parents' approval for her trip; in the Middle Ages respectable girls left home for only two reasons—either to marry or to enter a convent. Now, for the first time she told her parents about her voices and visions.

When she went on to explain what they had commanded her to do, her father, as she had feared, flatly refused to grant his permission. To his way of thinking, only girls with low morals traveled with soldiers. He forbade her to pay attention to her voices and declared he would rather drown her with his own hands than to see her undertake such a journey. Then, after having a dream about her attempting to leave home with soldiers, he persuaded another villager to claim that Joan had promised to marry him. Joan denied their engagement and refused to marry the man. Her supposed fiancé went so far as to sue her for breach of promise, but in arguing in her own defense, Joan was highly persuasive. The judge dismissed the case and praised her eloquence.

For children to defy their parents' wishes in the fifteenth century was almost unheard of, and it was especially hard for a good and pious girl like Joan to take such a step. Nevertheless, that is exactly what she determined to do in order to obey her voices. Since it was not possible for her to reach Baudricourt at Vaucouleurs on her own, she enlisted the aid of her cousin Durand Laxart.

Joan explained to Laxart that she intended to take the Dauphin to Reims, the city where France's kings were traditionally crowned. Laxart was naturally astonished, but she reminded him of the ancient, well-known prophecy that said that France would be lost by a woman and saved by a virgin. The first part, she reminded him, had already come about when the Dauphin's mother, Queen Isabelle, had sided with the Duke of Burgundy in convincing her husband to sign the Treaty of Troyes, giving France to the English king. Now, Joan told Laxart,

she was the maiden appointed by God to save France.

Vaucouleurs

Durand Laxart became Joan's first convert. Under her persuasion, he escorted her as she sought an audience with Baudricourt. The commander of the fort at Vaucouleurs was a rough no-nonsense soldier. Therefore, when the young girl, wearing a patched red dress and a kerchief, first appeared before him to tell him God had chosen her to save France, he dismissed her harshly. Telling Laxart to take her home, he also advised him to give Joan a good thrashing for her impertinence.

Joan was not discouraged. Her voices had warned her it would take several visits before Baudricourt would agree to help her. The second time Laxart took her to Vaucouleurs, early in 1429, she determined to wait the captain out and found lodging with the family of a wheelwright. Despite a second discouraging visit with the captain, she remained in Vaucouleurs.

While she waited, she prayed every day in the church of St. Mary, on the hill above the town. Her devotion became a topic of conversation among the inhabitants of the town who observed her kneeling before the statue of the Virgin Mary with her head bowed down in her hands or lifted up in passionate appeal. She also talked freely of her mission. As a result people began to look at her with both curiosity and awe. Her absolute belief in her mission also convinced more people that she was indeed the virgin in whose hands France's salvation rested.

One of her earliest and most faithful friends was Jean de Metz, a squire in Baudricourt's household. He later recalled how he had teased her at first, saying: "Honey, what are you doing here? Shouldn't the Dauphin be thrown out and all of us become English?" He also recalled Joan's reply:

I came here to the king's chamber [that is, into royal territory] to speak to Robert de Baudricourt so that he would either bring me or have me brought to the king, but he pays no attention to me or to my words; nevertheless, it is important that I be at the king's side before mid-Lent arrives, even if it means I have to walk until my feet are worn down to my knees; there is in fact, no one else, neither a king nor a duke . . . nor any other who can recover the kingdom of France, and he will have no help, if not through me, even though I would prefer to stay home and spin wool with my poor mother, for this is not my proper station, but I must go and I must do it, because my Lord wills that I do so.[6]

Another young squire in Baudricourt's household—Bertrand de Poulengy —also befriended Joan. He was acquainted with her family and was

willing to testify as to their good reputation. With these two well-respected soldiers to help plead her cause, Joan at last gained Baudricourt's reluctant permission to go to the Dauphin.

She quickly prepared to leave Vaucouleurs. Since a young woman traveling across the country would attract unwanted attention and harassment, she cut her dark hair short to resemble a man's. Sympathetic friends in Vaucouleurs supplied her with men's clothing suitable for the journey. Jean de Metz and Bertrand de Poulengy supplied other equipment, including boots and spurs as well as a horse. In addition to Metz and Poulengy and their two servants, her escort consisted of Colet de Vienne, a royal messenger who would be familiar with the route, and a man known as Richard the Archer. Late in the afternoon of February 23, 1429, this little band rode out from Vaucouleurs bound for Chinon and a meeting with the Dauphin.

Baudricourt went as far as the gate with them. In parting, he gave Joan a short sword suitable for her use and commended her to the care of her escort. Bidding her farewell he said, "Go! Go! And let come what will!"[7]

The Journey to Chinon
The distance from Vaucouleurs to Chinon was about 350 miles, much of it through hostile territory. Joan and her six companions made the trip in eleven days. They usually traveled by

In 1429 Joan traveled 350 miles across territory occupied by the English and Burgundians before reaching the Dauphin here at the castle of Chinon.

night and hid during the day, knowing that capture by roving bands of English or Burgundians might mean death. It was a cold journey through rough country, and often the travelers slept in the open. Although all the members of her escort were at least ten years older than she, Joan kept up their spirits. As well as or better than the hardened soldiers who were her escort, she endured the difficulties of the trip. Cold and wetness did not bother her nor did sleeping in stables or on the ground. Crossing rivers filled with chunks of ice did not faze her. Her sole complaint was that they were able to attend Mass only twice during the trip. She would have liked to stop at the church in every town through which they passed, but it would have been too risky.

Charles VII's Court

Although the Dauphin and his courtiers maintained a lavish lifestyle—as was expected in those times—he was actually deeply in debt. Records reveal that a butcher refused to supply meat to the royal kitchen and a cobbler refused to deliver shoes Charles had ordered because their bills had not been paid. Marguerite La Touroulde, wife of the king's receiver general, described the state of Charles' court (quoted in Mary Gordon's book Joan of Arc*):*

At that time there was in his kingdom and in those parts in obedience to the king such calamity and lack of money that it was piteous, and indeed those true to their allegiance to the king were in despair. I know it because my husband was at that time Receiver General and, of both the king's money and his own, he had not four crowns. And the city of Orléans was besieged by the English and there was no means of going to its aid. And it was in the midst of this calamity that Joan came, and I believe it firmly, she came from God and was sent to raise up the king and the people still within his allegiance for at that time there was no help but God.

King Charles VII spent enormous sums of money to maintain a lavish lifestyle for himself and his court.

Poulengy later described what it was like to travel in the company of their young leader:

> Every night she lay down with Jean de Metz and me, keeping upon her her surcoat and hose, tied and tight. I was young then and yet I had neither desire nor carnal movement to touch woman, and I should not have dared to ask such a thing of Joan, because of the abundance of goodness which I saw in her. . . . It seemed to me that she was sent by God, and I never saw in her any evil, but always was she so virtuous a girl that she seemed a saint.[8]

As they neared the end of their journey and entered friendly territory, the travelers were able to relax their vigilance. In the little village of Fierbois Joan attended Mass and prayed before the statue of St. Catherine three times in one day. There she also dictated a letter to be sent ahead to the Dauphin, telling him that she was coming to his aid.

Joan entered Chinon on March 6, 1429. It was the fourth Sunday in Lent, Laetare Sunday, when Joan and her young friends in Domremy used to picnic and hang garlands on the Fairies' Tree. On this day she was far from home and such innocent pleasures. In the distance she could see the magnificent towers of the castle of Chinon looming over the little town

on the banks of the river Vienne. In that castle resided the man whose kingdom she had come to save. As yet, however, she had no word from Charles and did not know if he would even receive her. While she waited for a reply she found lodgings with a respectable woman of the town.

The Meeting

News of Joan's arrival soon spread and a deputation of clergymen arrived to question her on behalf of the Dauphin. She refused to say anything to them except that she had two commands from God. The first was to relieve the city of Orléans, which was under siege by enemy forces, and the second was to take the Dauphin to Reims to be anointed and crowned. The questioners left, and the next evening, about dusk, she received word that the Dauphin would receive her.

She set out for the castle, and almost immediately came an event that many took as a sign that Joan was someone special. As she was about to cross the drawbridge, a mounted soldier stared at her and made a coarse, insulting remark, sprinkled with blasphemy. Joan turned to him and asked how he could blaspheme God when he was so near to death. Within an hour the man fell into the river and drowned. Whatever the cause of the accident, witnesses took it as a sign of Joan's power of prophecy.

The meeting between Joan and the Dauphin took place inside the castle in

What Joan Looked Like

Although numerous painters and sculptors have portrayed Joan, there is no authentic portrait or statue of her. In his book St. Joan of Arc, *John Beevers has summed up what can be gleaned about her appearance from stray remarks by contemporaries who mentioned her appearance and physical abilities:*

Although no authentic portrait of Joan of Arc exists, she is usually depicted as a stocky peasant girl with short-cropped black hair.

All we know of Joan is that her hair was black and cut short. Her complexion was dark and presumably sunburned and generally weather-beaten. She was rather short. There was nothing masculine about her voice; it was soft and womanly. She was strong, able to ride hard and long and wear armor for nearly a week at a stretch. No one ever said she was beautiful. She appears to have been a stocky peasant girl, used to hard work and the open air.

the great Hall of State. Some three hundred nobles crowded the room, which was lit by dozens of torches and a crackling fire in the immense fireplace. Most of those present were splendidly clothed in silks and velvets and rich robes—except for Charles, who wore a plain tunic. Despite his simple clothes, Joan recognized him, and bowing deeply before him said, "God send you long life, gentle Dauphin." When he asked her to explain before the assembly who she was and why she had come, she answered: "I am called Joan the Maid. I have been sent by God to take you to Reims to be anointed. Give me soldiers and I will raise the siege of Orléans, for it is God's will that the English shall leave France and return to their own country."[9]

In his biography of Joan, John Beevers gives an unflattering description of the twenty-six-year-old Charles at the time of this meeting:

In person, he was thin, with spindly, bandy legs, thick lips, watery eyes, and a long, bulbous nose. Both pious and superstitious, he heard three Masses a day and constantly consulted astrologers and soothsayers. He was cowardly and irresolute. Years later he became a good and able king, but at the time of his meeting with Joan, he was a pitiable specimen.[10]

When Charles asked Joan for proof that she was God's representative, she asked to speak to him alone. No one knows what was actually said during that conversation, but a persistent legend says that Joan told the Dauphin the details of a prayer he had made to God—a prayer that nobody would have overheard. Whatever was said, Charles was persuaded that Joan was what she said she was, and he arranged for her to stay in one of the castle's towers with a page and a lady to wait on her.

The Waiting Period

Although the Dauphin appeared to have been convinced by Joan, others in the court had not. Most of Charles's councillors and many high church offi-

cials connected with the court were outspoken in their doubts that this simple peasant girl represented God. In order to establish her credibility, messengers were sent to Domremy and Vaucouleurs to inquire about her reputation.

While Joan waited, she was visited by many people connected with the court. Some were clergy who bombarded her with repetitious questions, and others were courtiers who wanted to find out for themselves what this strange young woman was like. One of her visitors was the twenty-three-year-old Duke of Alençon, a relative of Charles's. He had spent five years as a prisoner in England and had only recently returned to France after being ransomed.

Alençon was one of the few in the court who immediately accepted Joan's story. He attended Mass with her and the Dauphin and dined with them. Afterward, they walked out into the meadows where he watched as Joan demonstrated her ability to handle a lance while on horseback—something a military leader would need to master. Alençon was so impressed by her skill that he immediately offered to make her the present of a fine horse. Joan happily accepted the gift and his invitation to spend four days at his castle with him and his young wife.

Impatient though she was to begin the work, as her voices were urging, Joan had to endure another searching examination. She was sent to Poitiers —a two-

Joan Answers the Professors

In Wilfred T. Jewkes and Jerome B. Landfield's *Joan of Arc*, there is an account of a portion of Joan's testimony at Poitiers. Among her examiners was Brother Seguin, a Carmelite friar who was dean of the faculty at Poitiers. He reported that when one interrogator stated: "You said the voice told you that God wishes to deliver the people of France from their present calamities. If He wishes to deliver them there is no need of soldiers," Joan replied, "In God's name, the soldiers will fight and God will give them the victory."

When Brother Seguin asked her what tongue her voice spoke, and she answered, "A better tongue than you do," he admitted, "And indeed I speak with a Limousin accent." And when Seguin asked her whether she believed in God, she answered, "Yes, more than you do."

Finally, when her examiners asked her for a sign that would prove that she was God's chosen representative, she exclaimed that although she did not know A from B, she knew God's will. "In God's name," she told them, "I have not come to Poitiers to make signs. But lead me to Orléans, and I will show the signs I was sent to make."

day ride from Chinon—to be questioned by renowned scholars from the University of Paris who had taken refuge there. The complete transcript of the proceedings at Poitiers has not survived, but bits and pieces of the questions and Joan's answers were later related by a Carmelite friar who was a leading member of the council that questioned her.

Her responses to the challenges thrown at her by the learned doctors, professors, and clergy show that she was not intimidated; in fact, she was cocky, sometimes humorous, and some-

times impatient with the inability of her learned questioners to understand the importance of her mission.

In the end the examiners concluded that she was a good Christian and recommended to the court that in view of the peril in which the town of Orléans stood, the Dauphin should accept her help. Although the hope of her being able to accomplish what the French generals had not been able to do was slender, she was the only hope available. At last Joan could make preparations to carry out her mission.

Chapter Three

Orléans Is Delivered

Joan of Arc's bold leadership and invincible courage—even after she was wounded in battle—inspired the French army to drive the entrenched enemy forces from the vicinity of Orléans. The freeing of Orléans was a major turning point in the French struggle to break the stranglehold the English/Burgundian allies had on the country.

Preparation for Battle

On March 22, 1429, before leaving Poitiers, Joan dictated an ultimatum to the king of England and the Duke of Bedford:

> Surrender to the Maid, who is sent here from God, the King of Heaven, the keys to all of the good cities that you have taken and vio-lated in France. . . . She is entirely ready to make peace, if you are willing to settle accounts with her, provided that you give up France and pay for having occupied her. And those among you, archers, companions-at-arms, gentlemen, and others who are before the city of Orléans, go back to your own countries, for God's sake. And if you do not do so, wait for the word of the Maid who will come visit you briefly to your great damage. . . . I am sent from God, the King of Heaven, to chase you all out of France. . . . If you do not wish to believe this message from God through the Maid, then wherever we find you we will strike you there, and make a great uproar greater than any made in France for a thousand years.[11]

Before Joan could head for Orléans, the Dauphin first sent her to Tours, a town famous for its armorers. There she waited to have a suit of armor made to fit her, staying at the home of Jean Dupuy, a respected citizen of the town. Joan's two brothers, Pierre and Jean, joined her. They told her that their mother had made a pilgrimage to the shrine of Puy to pray for Joan. Her brothers brought with them Jean Pasquerel, an Augustinian friar, whom Joan's mother had met in Puy and whom she recommended to Joan to serve as her chaplain and confessor (a priest whose main job is to hear confessions of sin and grant absolution). Joan liked him immediately,

The Maid's Armor

In her fitted armor Joan would have looked like a smaller version of a knight. Her cuirass, or body covering, was made up of several metal parts, including a breastplate, a back plate, and a skirt held together by straps, with chain armor filling in the gaps. Her leg coverings, were made up of pieces that allowed the knees to bend and shin guards; and her feet were covered by armored sollerets. There were six separate parts for each arm. At her request her *salade*, or steel helmet, was not fitted with a visor, as she wanted to be seen and heard by her soldiers. The entire outfit, which weighed about fifty pounds, required considerable help to get into or out of with all the pieces that had to be fitted to the body and straps that had to be fastened together.

Joan's suit of armor was unadorned, and looked nothing like the ornately decorated armor of the day.

and he joined the trusted attendants who formed her little retinue. In addition to the faithful Jean de Metz and Bertrand de Poulengy and Pasquerel, this retinue now included Joan's two brothers, two pages, and Jean d'Aulon, a squire assigned to her by the king to be her steward and companion.

A suit of armor, or "harness," had to be cut and fitted exactly in order to provide protection while restricting movement as little as possible. Joan's suit of armor was simple and plain, without the decorations found on the harnesses worn by knights. At Tours Joan also had a standard made for her to carry into battle. In designing the standard, she said she was following the counsel of her voices. On it was painted the image of God seated among clouds as the king of heaven, holding the world in one hand and the other raised in blessing. On either side of God knelt the angels Michael and Gabriel, each holding a fleur-de-lis (a stylized lily that was the emblem of the French king). In letters of gold were inscribed the words "Jhesus" and "Maria."

Accounts of Joan's stay in Tours tell of an occurrence that was seen as miraculous. Since every military leader carried a sword, Joan was offered one at Tours. However, she rejected the offer, saying she knew of a better one. Then she dictated a letter to the clergy in charge of the church of St. Catherine in Fierbois, where she had stopped on her way to Chinon. She

asked the priests to dig behind the altar to uncover a sword they would find there, one with five crosses engraved on it. According to reports of the time, the priests found the sword she described, covered with rust. After it was cleaned, however, it was in perfect condition. Historians have yet to find an explanation for how the sword might have ended up in such an unexpected location or how Joan knew where it was. Joan said only that her voices had told her where to find the sword she needed.

With the customary small battle-ax to complete her armaments, Joan moved on to the fortified town of Blois, located about halfway between Tours and Orléans. The Duke of Alençon was already there, busily assembling men and supplies for the attack on Orléans. At Blois Joan had a banner made bearing a painted image of Christ crucified, which she used as a rallying point for daily prayers during her campaigns.

Such daily prayers, conducted with the troops, were one indication of Joan's concern for the spiritual welfare of her soldiers. She insisted that in addition to attending twice-daily prayers, they go to confession and receive Communion. She also set strict standards of behavior. She would not allow gambling or profanity or prostitutes in the camps nor looting in the towns they captured. The Duke of Alençon testified:

Joan was chaste and she detested the women who follow soldiers. I saw her once . . . pursue with drawn sword a girl who was with the soldiers, and in such manner that in chasing her she broke her sword. She became very incensed when she heard the soldiers swear, and scolded them much and especially me who swore from time to time. So that when I saw her, I refrained from swearing.[12]

Because of her strong personality and charisma, Joan was able to change the ways not only of her "gentle duke" but also of the rough men she would lead into battle. One of the men who fell under her spell was a huge bear of a man called La Hire (the Angry One). Although he was famous for his bravery and for his robust oaths, he meekly submitted to her command that he use only her own expression "In God's name" or swear on his baton (a staff that was a symbol of his office).

On the Way to Orléans

On April 27, 1429, the royal army left Blois on its way to relieve the besieged city of Orléans. A band of clergy chanting "Come, Holy Spirit!" led the way. In full armor, surrounded by some of France's greatest warriors, Joan rode at the head of the company of between three and four thousand soldiers. Bringing up the rear were six hundred wagons loaded with provisions and arms and ammunition, trailed by a herd of four hundred cattle. Joan remained in her armor as they slept in the fields the first night out, and she awoke bruised and sore, unused to the weight of her metal harness.

Meanwhile the people of Orléans eagerly awaited the arrival of the rescue mission. The city, on the north bank of the Loire River, had been under siege by English forces for six months, and during that time refugees from the devastated countryside had swelled the population from about fifteen thousand to double that number. The city was greatly overcrowded, and although some supplies were slipped in past the enemy, these were not nearly enough to meet the needs of the citizens and soldiers camped within the walls.

The city's defenses had up to this point kept the enemy out. Thick walls thirty feet high surmounted by strong towers surrounded Orléans, which was entered by four gates. On the south side lay the river, spanned by a single bridge. The English had constructed a number of wooden forts (called bastilles) near the walls from which they could bombard the city. From time to time they sent great stone cannon balls crashing down on roofs, occasionally killing people. The large cannons, which launched the heavy stone balls, were called bombards. They were clumsy contraptions that were

Joan receives the sword of St. Catherine in this illustration. She claimed her voices told her that the sword was hidden behind the altar of the church of St. Catherine in Fierbois.

Joan's Leadership

Joan's position in the French army was peculiar. During her short military career she was never designated as the supreme commander of the army. The Dauphin told his officers to defer to her in everything, and yet they held councils and made decisions without consulting her. Some of the officers treated her as a divine mascot, but common soldiers and citizens hung on her every word and followed her lead without

question. She was not empowered to give orders, but her presence was enough to sway men to do as she wished. After the French military leaders saw that she was able to inspire the troops and lead them to victory, they also deferred to her decisions. And they as well as the troops accepted her unshakable belief that all of her actions were directed by God.

Although Joan was not officially empowered to give orders to the French army, both officers and soldiers deferred to her decisions.

loaded with gunpowder, which was ignited with a torch. Smaller cannons were difficult to aim accurately but did great damage when they hit their targets. There was also an occasional hand-to-hand encounter when guards or pickets met outside the gates. It seemed only a matter of time before the English brought in additional troops and breached the walls of the city with an all-out assault.

During the six-month standoff, word of the plight of Orléans had become known. The noted historian David Hume declares: "The eyes of all Europe were turned toward this scene where, it was reasonably supposed, the French were to make their last stand for maintaining the independence of their monarchy and the rights of their sovereign."[13] The people of the town had come to believe that only God could save them from being destroyed, so when they heard the rumors that Joan the Maid was sent by God they rejoiced.

Skirmishes

Joan's arrival at Orléans was stormy, both literally and figuratively. Heavy rain fell from black clouds. Joan was tired and furious because the French army leaders had thwarted her plan, which had been to march straight to a confrontation with the English leaders and demand their surrender. Instead, the French captains had detoured the troops and supplies past Orléans to Crécy, a village about five miles beyond the besieged city. From there they planned to float the convoy downstream to enter Orléans through the east gate, the one least strongly guarded by the enemy. Joan, who had not been informed of the plan and did not know the terrain, felt she had been tricked.

The commander of the French forces at Orléans was Jean Dunois, the son of the murdered Duke of Orléans. He was known as "the Bastard" because his mother was never married to the duke, but no shame was attached in those days to the offspring who resulted from such relationships. When the twenty-six-year-old knight, who was famous for his bravery and for his chivalry, hurried to welcome Joan, she rebuked him for what she saw as his interference in God's work. Dunois made a record of their conversation:

"Are you the Bastard of Orleans?"

"Yes, I am, and I rejoice in your coming."

"Are you the one who gave orders for me to come here, on this side of the river, so that I could not go directly to Talbot and the English?"

I answered that I and others, including the wisest men around me, had given this advice, believing it best and safest; then Joan said to me, "In God's name, the counsel of Our Lord God is wiser and safer than yours. You thought you could fool me, and instead you fool yourself; I bring you better help than ever came to any soldier to any city. It is the help of the King of Heaven."[14]

Dunois expressed concern that a strong wind was coming from the wrong direction and the flotilla of barges assembled at Orléans could not sail upstream to pick up the supplies brought by the convoy. Joan told him not to worry, that the wind would change. Then, according to Dunois's account, the wind suddenly changed and became favorable.

Sails were therefore raised, and I brought in the ships and rafts. . . . From that moment I had great hopes of [Joan], greater than before, and I begged her to cross the

Loire and enter the city of Orléans where they were most eager for her. . . . Then Joan came with me, carrying her white standard. . . . And she crossed the river with La Hire and me, and we entered the town of Orléans together.[15]

When Joan entered Orléans about eight o'clock on the evening of April

The citizens of Orléans crowd around Joan as she enters the city in April 1429. The people welcomed her as a savior who would deliver them from the English.

29, 1429, the wildly cheering citizens, carrying torches that lit up the night, turned out to greet her. Church bells pealed joyously as people rushed to touch her stirrup or her banner. After visiting a church to give thanks for her safe arrival, she took up lodgings in the house of Jacques Boucher, the town's treasurer. At last she took off her armor, and after eating a little bread dipped in wine and water, she went to bed.

The Week of the Deliverance

The next day Joan met with the French military leaders. Some were for attacking the English bastilles immediately, and others wanted to wait for reinforcements. Joan insisted on giving the English a chance to withdraw peaceably. Twice she went out on the ramparts facing enemy bastilles and shouted to the English, urging them to surrender or she would be forced to drive them out. And twice she got back insults and threats that they would burn her when they got hold of her.

The following day, May 1, was Sunday. An anonymous contemporary account, *The Journal of the Siege of Orléans*, describes what happened on that day:

> The people of Orléans had such great desire to see Joan the Maid that they almost broke down the gate of her lodging in order to see her; therefore that day she rode on horseback throughout the city, accompanied by many knights and squires; there were so many city people in the streets through which she was riding that she was scarcely able to pass, for the people could not have their fill of seeing her.[16]

On Monday and Tuesday while waiting for more French troops to arrive, Joan inspected the English fortifications and made plans. She also went to a church near her lodging, where she assisted with the Mass and prayed for the relief of the city. Early on Wednesday morning she rode out with five hundred soldiers to welcome the French reinforcements and escort them into the city. By noon they were all safely inside the gates, and Joan sat down to have dinner with her squire, d'Aulon.

While they were eating, Dunois came with the news that Sir John Fastolf, an English hero of the Battle of Agincourt, was on his way with provisions and reinforcements for the enemy. Joan reacted happily to the news. "In God's name, Bastard," she said, "I charge you to let me know as soon as you hear of his arrival. Should he pass without my knowledge—I will have your head!"[17] Dunois assured her she would have the news the instant it came.

A short time later as Joan was resting, she suddenly sprang up, crying that her voices were warning her that French blood was being shed. Hastily donning her armor, she mounted her horse. Witnesses who saw her said she rode so fast her horse's hooves struck showers of sparks from the cobblestones. Upon investigating, Joan found that a skirmish was underway about a mile and a half from the city at the Bastille de Saint-Loup, a monastery that the English had captured and fortified.

When Joan arrived at Saint-Loup, the French attackers were being driven back by the English defenders and had begun to stream back toward the city. Joan rallied the retreating soldiers, urging them to follow her. The French soldiers turned about and attacked so furiously that the English formations wavered, broke, and fled back into the fort. The French soldiers stormed the fort, killing at least 114 English. The fortification was burned to the ground, but Joan would not allow the church to be burned. Only two Frenchmen were killed. The victory was important because Orléans was now open to the east.

The skirmish was Joan's first taste of battle, and she wept for the English who had been killed without having been cleansed of their sins by confession. She herself went immediately to confession and urged the French soldiers to confess their sins and give thanks to God for the victory. The next day was Ascension Thursday (celebrating the rising of Christ into heaven) and Joan refused to make war on that holy day. After going to Mass and confession, she sent the English a final warning letter:

You, O English, who have no right to this kingdom of France, the King of Heaven orders and commands you through me, Joan the Maid, to leave your fortresses and return to your country, and if you do not so I shall make a *hahay* [uproar] that will be perpetually remembered. Behold I write you for the third and final time; I shall write you no further.

Jesus-Maria, Joan the Maid.[18]

Since the English had violated the unwritten laws of warfare by taking her last herald prisoner, she had this letter tied to an arrow and shot across the river to them. When they replied to it with shouted insults and taunts, she wept and called on God to help her.

The next day, Friday, Joan took part in the attack on the Bastille des Augustins, where the English had fled after the fall of Saint-Loup. With La Hire at her side she led the forces that stormed the fort. The English defended fiercely, but the French attacked more fiercely, and the English in des Augustins were killed, taken prisoner, or made their escape to the fortress called the Bastille des Tourelles.

At one point Joan dismounted and was wounded in the foot when she stepped on a caltrop—one of the spiked metal balls scattered on the ground to disable the attackers' horses. It was only a minor wound, but she told her confessor Jean Pasquerel that she would suffer a more serious wound

Joan carries her standard as she leads the charge into battle. During the battle at the Bastille de Saint-Loup, Joan rallied the retreating French forces and led them to victory.

The English View of Joan

At the time of the fall of Orléans, Henry V's younger brother, the Duke of Bedford, (acting as regent for the infant Henry VI) was the overall head of the English forces in France. He blamed the English defeat at Orléans on the devil. He tried to explain to the people back in England what had happened in a letter probably written in July 1429. In Saint Joan of Arc *Vita Sackville-West quotes a fragment of this letter:*

> There fell, by the hand of God, as it seemeth, a great stroke upon your people that was assembled there [at Orléans] in great number, caused in great part, as I trow, of lack of sad belief and unlawful doubt that they had a disciple and limb of the Fiend, called the Pucelle, that used false enchantments and sorcery. That which stroke and discomfiture not only lessened in great part the number of your people there, but as well withdrew the courage from the remnant in marvelous wise.

In that superstitious age, everything was black or white with no shades of gray. You were either under the control of God or of the devil. Clearly, in English minds, Joan was now firmly fixed as a disciple of the devil. In several of their numerous encounters with her, various English fighters swore to capture and burn her as a witch.

the next day. She also asked him to stay close by her the next day as she would have much to do.

For six months the fortress of the Tourelles had blocked the bridge leading into Orléans. On May 7, over the opposition of many of the French leaders, Joan insisted on attacking the entrenched English forces there. The battle lasted from early morning until sunset. About noon Joan was struck by an arrow that embedded itself above her breast. Crying with frustration, she withdrew from the fight to have the arrow removed. After the wound was treated in customary fashion by smearing it with bacon fat and olive oil, she returned to the fight.

The sight of their wounded leader returning to battle gave renewed courage to the soldiers. But when the fighting still continued as night was falling, Dunois wanted to withdraw the French troops into the city. Joan urged him to let the men have a brief rest and then renew the attack. She herself retired to a vineyard for about a quarter of an hour to pray. Then, in the dramatic climax to the battle, she grasped her standard and waving it vigorously rallied the men for a final ferocious assault. The Bastille des Tourelles was taken. With the loss of this stronghold, the next day the English retreated.

The long siege of Orléans was ended. The deliverance of the city was a major victory for the French in their fight to free themselves from foreign domination; from that time on their deliverer would be known as The Maid of Orléans.

Chapter Four

THE GLORIOUS SPRING

Lifting the siege of Orléans made it possible for the Dauphin to go to Reims to be crowned. In escorting France's monarch to Reims, Joan of Arc fulfilled the second part of the mission assigned her by her voices. This achievement brought her to the height of her power and popularity.

To Crown a King

When the siege was lifted the people of Orléans were beside themselves with joy. They were ready to worship Joan as their savior, but she refused to accept their thanks for herself, instead telling them to offer their thanksgiving to God. On May 10, as she left the city which she had first entered ten days earlier, the people pressed up to her, offering gifts and trying to kiss her hands and feet.

Joan was anxious to reach the Dauphin, but her wound from the English arrow was still troublesome, so when she arrived at Blois she rested there for two days. Then she hurried on to meet the Dauphin, who had come from Chinon to honor her for delivering Orléans. When they met outside of Tours, Joan rode up to Charles and bowed low, but he raised her up and embraced her. Together they rode to the castle where the court was staying. Joan was treated as an honored guest, with comfortable quarters and many servants, but that was not what she wanted. Her goal now was to take the Dauphin to Reims to be crowned, and anything that delayed attaining that goal only annoyed her.

There were several reasons for the delay in starting for Reims. As usual, Charles hesitated while he listened to the advice of his counselors. Several of his most intimate advisers had vested interests in delaying the coronation. The uncrowned Dauphin was more dependent on them than he would be as the crowned king, and they were not inclined to give up the power that the Dauphin's dependence gave them. There was also the fact that English forces occupied a number of towns on the way to Reims, which lay deep in the English-held region of Champagne. Finally, there was the question of whether it would be better to follow up

Joan kneels before the Dauphin Charles outside Tours. After lifting the siege of Orléans, Joan escorted the Dauphin to the city of Reims to be crowned king.

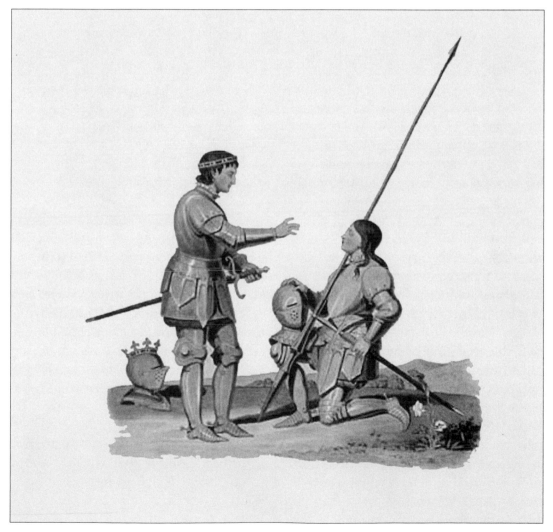

Joan's Strategy

Some historians and biographers have argued that Joan would have been wiser to follow up the liberation of Orléans by marching to Paris instead of insisting on escorting the Dauphin to Reims to be crowned. Not only would that strategy not have been in accordance with the instructions of her voices, it also would not have been in accordance with medieval thinking. Kings in those days were considered to have superhuman power—but only after they had been anointed and consecrated. In his book St. Joan of Arc *John Beevers writes:*

> Within his [the king's] own sphere, he was God's regent and at the coronation ceremony he pledged himself to God and was accepted by God and consecrated by His priests. He only entered into the fullness of his kingship with this consecration. Not one of Joan's fellow citizens would ever have considered Charles as true King until his crowning. Those Frenchmen loyal to his cause accepted him as the lawful heir to the throne of France, the man who had the right to be crowned, but in their eyes he had not stepped over that mystic line which separated him from his subjects and placed him in a wholly different category of human beings. That irrevocable step could be taken only in the Cathedral of Rheims.

the Orléans victory with an all-out push to free Paris before taking time for a journey to Reims for what, after all, was a symbolic ceremony.

In Joan's mind there was no doubt that the crowning ceremony was essential to increasing the power of the king and diminishing the power of the enemy, since this was what her voices kept telling her. Relentlessly she badgered Charles to proceed immediately to Reims. Dunois, who had accompanied her to Tours, described how she burst into a meeting between the Dauphin and his royal council: "The

Maid, before entering the chamber, knocked on the door and as soon as she entered she dropped to her knees and embraced the legs of the king, saying these words or others like them: 'Do not hold a council meeting for such a long time, but come as quickly as possible to Reims to receive a worthy crown.'"[19]

The Loire Campaign

Soon after this meeting the Dauphin agreed to leave for Reims, using troops to oust the English from their strongholds on the banks of the Loire River. Joan was pleased when the Dauphin made her faithful friend the Duke of Alençon lieutenant general in charge of the royal army, and she promised Alençon's wife that she would bring him back to her safely. Now that she was free to act, Joan moved quickly.

The first objective of the royal army was the English-held town of Jargeau, which was about twelve miles east of Orléans. Held by the Earl of Suffolk, it was important to take Jargeau before English reinforcements and supplies reached it. The French marched first to Orléans, where upon her return Joan received a joyous welcome, provisions and munitions, and an additional two thousand soldiers, raising the total number of the royal army to over four thousand.

On the evening of June 11, when the French forces approached Jargeau, the English came out to meet them. As the battle began, Joan seized her standard and rode into the middle of the melee, calling encouragement to the soldiers. When the English retired into the city at nightfall, the French camped in the suburbs of Jargeau.

The next morning the French captains as usual wanted to hold a council to discuss plans, but Joan had no intention of spending hours in discussions when she could be attacking. She rallied the Duke of Alençon, who reported their conversation: "Joan said, 'Forward gentle duke to the assault! . . . Have no doubt, the hour that pleases God is at hand. . . . Act and God will act!' She said to me later, 'Are you afraid, gentle duke? Do you not know that I promised your wife to bring you back safe and sound?'"[20]

The assault began according to Joan's wishes. Once again seeming miracles occurred in her presence. Seeing the Duke of Alençon holding a certain position, she told him to move from that spot before a cannonball hit him. He did as she told him, and a cannonball killed another knight who had moved to the spot where the duke had been.

At another point in the battle, while Joan was on a scaling ladder with her standard in her hand, a stone hit the flag and broke into pieces as it ricocheted onto her helmet. Nearby soldiers gasped in horror as she crashed to the ground in her heavy armor, but in an instant she sprang up crying, "Up, up my friends! Our Lord has condemned the English, at this very hour they are ours; take courage!"[21] The French did take courage. In the renewed assault Suffolk was taken prisoner, and the surviving English retreated from Jargeau.

When Joan and Alençon rode back to Orléans she found a gift waiting for her from the Duke of Orléans. It was a fine cloak of scarlet and a tunic of deep green (the colors of the House of Orléans) that could be worn over her armor. Although she wore men's clothing and armor because they were practical for the life she was leading, Joan loved bright colors and rich materials, and she was delighted with the present.

There was no time for dallying in Orléans, however; Joan urged the army to continue its mission to clear the road to Reims. Following the capture of Jargeau, the towns of Meung and Beaugency capit- ulated without much of a struggle. Realizing the Loire campaign was over, the English began to retreat toward Paris. French troops led by La Hire hotly pursued their objective to force a decisive battle.

During the battle for the town of Jargeau, a number of seeming miracles occurred in Joan's presence that helped the French achieve victory.

The Sacred Oil

Reims lies on the Vesle River about one hundred miles northeast of Paris. Built in the 1200s, the cathedral of Notre Dame de Reims is one of the most beautiful examples of Gothic architecture. The magnificence of the church and the beauty of the setting were not, however, the reason it had been the place where all French kings were crowned. As Joan and every other French citizen knew, it was the tiny crystal flask containing the precious drops of holy oil kept in the city that mattered. According to legend, in 496, when St. Remy baptized and anointed King Clovis, the first Christian king of France, a white

dove descended from heaven with the holy oil. Supposedly the amount of oil in the flask never changed—no matter how often it was used. As Joan watched the archbishop mark Charles with the holy oil on his head, chest, shoulders, elbows, and wrists, she (and all the other witnesses) believed Charles was being filled with the Holy Spirit.

From the fifth century, the coronation ceremony for the kings of France took place in the cathedral of Notre Dame de Reims.

The Battle of Patay

The battle the French wanted occurred on the morning of June 18. Previously Joan had predicted that the French that day would win their greatest victory, and she was right. The Battle of Patay became for the French their revenge for the Battle of Agincourt. Two outstanding generals, Lord Talbot and John Fastolf, headed the English forces.

Their strategy was to have five hundred archers under Talbot take up positions among the thick hedges near Patay. There, hidden from the approaching French soldiers, they planned to defend the narrow passageway while their rear guard gathered for battle.

The French sent out skirmishers to try to locate the enemy. As the scouts cautiously searched for the well-hidden

English soldiers, a deer suddenly bolted out of the woods and ran toward the English formation. The archers did not realize that the French were near. Excited by the unexpected appearance of the deer, a number of the archers cheered and gave the traditional English hunting cry of "View Halloo!" The French scouts heard the cries and raced back to report the enemy's position.

As a result of this turn of fortune, the French cavalry was able to attack before the English had finished their preparations. The French horsemen rushed past the archers to destroy the main force of the English army. The battle quickly became a rout and then a massacre. Fastolf retreated and Talbot was captured. Reports of the number of English casualities differ, but over two thousand were killed while only a handful of French lives were lost.

Although Joan had been eager for the fight to begin, she was distressed when the battle turned into a massacre. One of her pages reported: "She was most pitiful at the sight of so great a slaughter. A Frenchman was leading some English prisoners; he struck one of them on the head; the man fell senseless. Joan sprang from her saddle and held the Englishman's head in her lap, comforting him; and he was shriven [forgiven his sins]."[22] Her concern for the dying English soldier was typical of her behavior in all the battles she took part in. She hated the killing but was convinced it was necessary to save France.

The Road to Reims

News of the glorious victories at Orléans and Patay spread throughout France, and thousands of Frenchmen rushed to join the royal army. They were eager to help free their country under the leadership of the Maid and also to accompany their Dauphin to his crowning. The future king, however, was apparently not as eager. Again he hesitated, moving around from castle to castle with his councillors. Joan followed the royal court from place to place, reminding the reluctant prince that her voices had warned her that her time to act was brief and begging him to make use of her. Finally the Dauphin yielded to the popular enthusiasm and to Joan's relentless pressure. On June 29 he set out with his royal court to follow the Maid to Reims.

The first important city they came to was Auxerre, a city loyal to the Duke of Burgundy. The city's leaders offered to pay two thousand pieces of gold and provide provisions for the troops in order not to be attacked. Joan wanted to boldly take the town and force its obedience to the future king, but the Dauphin's advisers prevailed. Over her protests the bribe was accepted, and the royal army skirted around the city.

At Saint-Florentin they were received hospitably, but the rulers of the important city of Troyes were not prepared to yield. The reason was largely economic. Troyes was a cloth-manufacturing city and depended on the goodwill of the English and Burgundians to market its goods. Again the Dauphin's advisers tried to persuade him to bypass the city, but this time Joan insisted that the citizens be made to recognize their rightful ruler. An eyewitness described what happened:

At the moment when the King was before the town of Troyes, and while the soldiers saw that they had no more victuals and were discouraged and ready to withdraw, Joan told the King that he should doubt not and that on the morrow he would have the town. Then she took her standard; many foot soldiers followed her to whom

Report to the Queen

Charles's wife, Marie of Anjou, was not at his crowning. Because of the danger involved in traveling to Reims, he had sent her back to Bourges. He did arrange for a report of the ceremony to be sent to her. In Joan of Arc: Her Story *Regine Pernoud and Marie Veronique Clin record a part of the report to the queen:*

And at the hour that the king was consecrated and also when they had placed the crown on his head, every man cried out: Noel! and the trumpets sounded so that it seemed as though the walls of the church should have crumbled. During the aforesaid mystery, the Maid was always at the king's side, holding his standard in her hand. It was fine to see the elegant manners not only of the king but also of the Maid, and God knows that you would have wished them well.

Holding her standard, Joan of Arc stands in full armor at the altar of the cathedral at Reims during the coronation of King Charles VII in July 1429.

she gave order to make faggots [bundles of sticks] to fill the moats. They made many of them, and on the morrow Joan cried the assault, signifying that they should put the faggots into the moats. Seeing this, the inhabitants of Troyes, fearing attack, sent to the King to negotiate a composition [agreement]. And the King made composition with the inhabitants and made his entry into Troyes in great pomp, Joan carrying her standard beside the King.[23]

On July 14 the entourage reached Chalons, where Charles was presented with the keys to the city and welcomed joyously. Here Joan was happy to meet several friends from Domremy, including one of her godfathers, who had journeyed to Chalons to join in the procession to Reims for the coronation. In response to letters of invitation sent by the Dauphin, hundreds of other well-wishers from many other towns also came to join the royal party on the final stage of its journey to Reims.

On the evening of July 16 Charles the Dauphin made his formal entry into the city of Reims to wild acclaim. The next day, Sunday, July 17, 1429, he was anointed with holy oil and crowned with awe-inspiring ceremony in the majestic cathedral of Notre Dame de Reims. Amid the splendidly robed participants was one woman, Joan, wearing a white silk tunic over her suit of armor.

During the ceremony Joan stood beside the Dauphin, holding her standard, to which she attached great importance. When asked why she alone carried an unfurled standard into the cathedral, she replied: "It had borne the burden; it had earned the honor."[24] After the ceremony Joan knelt before the newly crowned king and said to him, "Gentle king, from this moment the pleasure of God is executed. He wished me to raise the siege of Orleans and bring you to the city of Reims to receive your anointing, which shows that you are the true king and the one to whom the kingdom should belong."[25] Many of the spectators wept with joy. It was Joan of Arc's finest hour.

Chapter Five

From Reims to Paris

Following the coronation that her efforts had made possible, Joan became a national heroine. She decided to take advantage of her fame and power by leading the French army to Paris and finally driving the English from French soil. But powerful forces—even within the king's court—opposed her. More ominously, her voices were less clear on what her course of action should be.

Intrigue

Following the crowning of the king, Joan anticipated that the next logical step in recovering France from the enemy would be to take Paris. At this point, however, political intrigue took the place of military valor in determining the course of events for France and her king. Three weeks before the ceremony she had sent word to the Duke of Burgundy urging him to attend the coronation and take his place among the nobles at the altar when the king was anointed. Since he had not replied, on the day of the crowning she had sent another message:

> Joan the Maid, in the name of the King of Heaven, requires you and the King of France to make a good and lasting peace. . . . Forgive one another entirely as becomes good Christians. . . . Prince of Burgundy, I pray you, I entreat you as humbly as I can not to make war any longer against the holy realm of France, and speedily to withdraw your men from the strongholds and fortresses of the said holy kingdom.[26]

As Joan's second letter was on its way, envoys from the Duke of Burgundy and his English ally, the Duke of Bedford, arrived in Reims. They had come, they said, to negotiate a truce. Unknown to Joan, the king's chief councillor Georges de la Trémoille had been working behind the scenes with the Duke of Burgundy. La Trémoille hoped to recover Paris without a battle. If he were successful, he instead of Joan would get credit for freeing the capital city.

Following Charles's coronation, Joan resolved to retake Paris and drive the English permanently from France.

The King's Favor

Among those attending the coronation were Joan's father and Durand Laxart, the relative who had believed in her enough to twice escort her to Vaucouleurs. The two men were provided with comfortable living quarters in Reims and honored by the court. Joan, far from acting the part of someone worshipped by her nation, was still the warmhearted girl who had left Domremy only five months earlier. When Charles VII asked Joan what he could do for her to show his gratitude, the only favor she asked was that he free the people of Domremy from taxes forever, and the king gave her father a document freeing the inhabitants of Domremy from all taxes. That pledge would be honored for another 360 years, until the French Revolution removed the French monarchy from power.

La Trémoille and other royal councillors did their best to keep Joan ignorant of what went on in their secret meetings. When she finally learned that they had made a fifteen-day truce with the English and their Burgundian allies, she was dismayed. She did not believe that the Duke of Burgundy would surrender Paris peacefully at the end of the truce period. In her view the truce was a delaying tactic to gain time for more English troops to be sent to the area. The only reason she would respect the truce was, she said, to preserve the king's honor.

A Time of Frustration

The coronation of Charles VII changed the mood of the country from one of despair to one of hope. The people had reason to believe that the despised enemy would soon be gone. Both Charles VII and Joan shared this belief,

but they expected it to happen by different means. Joan, distrusting the English and the Duke of Burgundy, argued for a swift all-out assault to free Paris before enemy reinforcements reached the city. But the weak king preferred to listen to those among his councillors who advised against military action.

Instead of undertaking a march on Paris, King Charles VII set out on a triumphal tour. Now that he was a true king, city officials along the way wanted to recognize him and express their joy by giving him the keys to their cities and entertaining him lavishly. Joan, too, was honored, but although she was pleased by the acclaim showered on her by the people, she began to feel her usefulness to her country was over. "Please God, my Maker," she told Dunois, "that I may now withdraw myself, leave off arms, and go and serve my father and my mother by keeping the sheep with my sister and my brothers who will rejoice so greatly to see me again."[27]

Joan's hopes for returning to her village were soon dashed as her distrust of the English was borne out. Four thousand English troops landed in northern France and headed for Paris. And during the first week in August, the Duke of Bedford, who was ruling France on behalf of Henry VI, the infant king of England, sent Charles a letter challenging him to meet in combat. The tone of the letter was insulting. Bedford accused Charles of falsely calling himself king and of deceiving the people of France "with the aid of superstitious and damnable persons such as a woman of a disorderly and infamous life and dissolute manners dressed in the clothes of a man."[28]

At the Gates of Paris

For several weeks there were inconclusive skirmishes between French and English forces within a radius of fifty miles of Paris. Joan grew increasingly impatient, and finally told Alençon they *must* go to Paris. On August 23, with a picked company, she and the duke set out for Saint-Denis, five miles north of Paris. She was eager to examine the terrain in the area and decide on the best plan for attacking the walls of the capital.

Joan and Alençon repeatedly sent messages to the king, begging him to join them with his troops in Saint-Denis, but he held back. In fact, Charles was busily undermining their plans. In August Charles and La Trémoille concluded a truce with the enemy that was supposed to last until Christmas.

Unaware of the existence of this document, at noon on Thursday, September 8, Joan led a large company of soldiers in an attack on the Saint-Honore gate of Paris. There were several obstacles to overcome before the gate could be reached. These included a dry trench at least ten feet deep, a mound of earth, and a water-filled moat more than sixty feet wide. After the attackers swarmed through the dry trench and up onto the earthen mound, there was a lively exchange of fire with the defenders of the city. An eyewitness reported:

> The Maid took her standard in hand and with the first troops entered the ditches toward the swine market. The assault was hard and long, and it was wondrous to hear the noise and the explosion of the cannons and the culverins [crude firearms] that those inside the city fired against those outside, and all manner of blows in such great abundance that they were beyond being counted.[29]

There was no bridge over the moat at this point, so Joan had the soldiers make bundles of sticks to fill it. But it soon became evident that the amount of wood would not be adequate to bridge the moat.

In this page from an illuminated manuscript, Joan leads the assault on Paris. During the doomed siege, Joan was wounded in the thigh by a bolt from an English crossbow.

Then Joan went along the edge of the moat checking the depth of the water with her lance, trying to find a shallow place where it could be crossed. While she was concentrating on this task, a bolt from an English crossbow struck her on the thigh, hitting her with such force that it split the steel plate of her armor and penetrated her flesh. As she was being carried to shelter behind the mound, she urged the men to continue fighting. Night had fallen, though, and the soldiers were weary. Two knights carried her to a shelter some distance from the battlefield, despite her protest, "In God's name, the city might have been ours!"[30]

The next day Joan had herself placed in her saddle and started with Alençon toward Paris to renew the assault. The French had bridged the Seine River, and she hoped it would provide an easier way into the city. Very soon a messenger arrived to say that the king had had the bridge destroyed and had ordered the French army to retreat to Saint-Denis. The assault on Paris was ended by royal decree.

The Wasted Months

With the assault on Paris abandoned, the army disintegrated. In addition, Joan's best supporters and friends at court disappeared. Dunois and La Hire departed on other assignments, and Alençon returned to his estate—safe and sound, as Joan had promised. The king refused Alençon's petition to allow Joan to accompany him.

Symbol and Substance

In *Joan of Arc* Mary Gordon discusses the importance of Joan as a symbol of victorious rescue. Gordon points out that Joan understood herself as a symbolic figure and also realized the symbolic nature of her mission. When Charles VII was unable or unwilling to provision and pay her soldiers during the bitterly cold winter of 1429, the hungry, freezing soldiers began to desert in large numbers. "Her defeats," Gordon says, "occurred when symbolic action was insufficient, when the reality drowned the image and the dream. She couldn't make it [the campaign to take Paris] work on air forever."

Joan of Arc has become an enduring symbol of victorious rescue for the French.

When the king moved to his castle at Bourges, Joan stayed for three weeks in the home of the receiver general of the town. His wife, Marguerite La Touroulde, gave this report of her guest:

She behaved like an honest and Christian woman. She went to confession very often, loved to hear Mass, and often asked me to go to Matins [a church service, usually held in the early morning]. . . . I remember some women coming to the house while Joan was living there. They brought rosaries and other holy objects for her to touch. She burst out laughing and said to me, "You touch them! Your touch is just as good as mine." She was very generous in almsgiving and was always giving money to the needy. She said she had been sent to comfort the poor and destitute.[31]

As king and court wandered from one chateau to another, Joan trailed along, restless and unhappy. The king was enjoying living a courtly life, and he and his chief adviser, La Trémoille, did not want to stir up Burgundy or the English. But like a gadfly, Joan pestered them to allow her to save France. Finally, at the end of October it was decided that an attempt should be made to reclaim two small towns from the Burgundians. One of them was Saint-Pierre and the other was La Charité.

Saint-Pierre and La Charité

Saint-Pierre was a well-fortified town, placed high on a steep bluff over the river Allier. With a small, hastily gathered army Joan and the French commander Charles de Albret bombarded it for a week. When a breach was made in the wall, orders were given to attack, but the town was well garrisoned, and the defenders easily repulsed the attackers. The French retreat was already underway when Joan's steward Jean d'Aulon saw her standing at the edge of the moat outside the town with a few men around her.

Alarmed, he asked what she was doing there practically alone, and she replied that she had a host of fifty

House of Burgundy

Joan's fortunes and fate were entwined with the fortunes of three Dukes of Burgundy. Before she was born, Philip the Bold (1342–1404) had married Margaret, heiress of Flanders and other countries in the lowlands (including what is now the Netherlands, Belgium, and much of northern France). This alliance ensured that his heirs would be the richest princes in Christendom, as well as the most powerful.

His son, John the Fearless (1371–1419) was eager for conflict and conquest. In 1407 he arranged for the assassination of his first cousin, the Duke of Orléans. In turn, the Orléans faction arranged for the assassination of John the Fearless. It happened on September 10, 1419, during a parley between John the Fearless and the Dauphin—the future Charles VII. These murders led to an ever-widening gulf between Charles and the House of Burgundy.

Duke John's son Philip (1396–1467) was twenty-three when he inherited the title to the ducal estate of Burgundy. He had grand plans for expanding his vast territory and, some historians say, for establishing a separate kingdom to rule over. His alliance with England helped to further his ambitions. When Joan appeared on the scene and lifted the siege of Orléans and then insisted on taking the reluctant Dauphin to Reims to be crowned, she must have seemed a tremendous threat to him and to his grandiose plans.

After the aborted campaign to retake Paris, Joan led a small army in an attempt to capture two small towns from the Burgundians.

thousand with her. Historians have assumed that Joan was referring to a vision she was experiencing. The steward was not a believer in supernatural beings, for he reported:

At that time, despite what she said, she did not have with her more than four or five men. . . . I said to her directly that she should leave and retire as the others had done; and then she said that I should bring some bundles of sticks and wicker hurdles to make a bridge over the town moat so that they could approach better. Having just given me that instruction, she cried out in a loud voice: "To the bundles and hurdles, everybody, make the bridge!" —which was prepared swiftly and then accomplished. I was entirely amazed, for the city was taken all at once by her assault, without finding therein very much resistance.[32]

After the fall of Saint-Pierre, Joan headed north toward La Charité with her little army. Their supply of munitions and supplies was dangerously low. The siege of La Charité, which began in bitterly cold weather on November 14, was not successful. In addition to munitions, the French besiegers were short of men and the money to pay their wages, and Charles VII made no effort to send aid of any kind. After a month the siege had to be lifted, and Joan unhappily withdrew.

Despite this failure, during this winter Joan received several honors. The king conferred nobility on her and her family:

Wishing to give thanks for the multiple and striking benefits of divine grandeur that have been accorded us through the agency of the Maid d'Ay de Domremy. . . considering also the praiseworthy, graceful, and useful services already rendered by the aforesaid Joan the Maid in every way, to us and to our kingdom, which we hope to pursue in the future.[33]

Her brothers had new shields made bearing the new logo and called themselves "d'Ay." Titles and a coat of arms and special privileges did not impress Joan, however.

Joan had a warm relationship with the people of Orléans, and as often as she could she visited the city she had delivered from its would-be captors. On January 19, 1430, the city council of Orléans presented her with a house in the town and gave her a banquet that included 52 pints of wine, 6 capons, 9 partridges, 13 rabbits, and a pheasant.

Joan was gratified to have the people she had helped express their thanks, but it was action, not honors, she craved. She was constantly aware that the year her heavenly advisers repeatedly told her she would have to accomplish her mission was growing very short.

Chapter Six

CAPTURE AND IMPRISONMENT

During the winter of 1429 and early spring of 1430, King Charles VII kept Joan at his side while he tried in vain to negotiate a peace. In the meantime the English and Burgundian invaders received reinforcements and became stronger. When Joan was finally permitted to act, she had too little in the way of men and arms, and it was too late to attempt to rout the enemy without putting herself in great personal danger.

An Uneasy Spring

Joan spent much of the winter of 1429 in anguished prayer vigils, knowing that time was running out for her as she languished with the court in the town of Sully on the Loire. Finally in late March or early April Joan left the court accompanied by her steward Jean d'Aulon, her brother Pierre, and four or five lancers. At Lagny a small band of soldiers joined them, and they rode on toward Paris. About Easter, April 16, they approached the town of Melun, which had been under Anglo-Burgundian control for many years. When the citizens heard that La Pucelle (The Maid) was outside their walls, they rose up against the enemy garrison and drove them out of the town. Then they threw open their gates and welcomed the Maid with great rejoicing.

It was while she was standing on a rampart at Melun, looking toward Paris, that she learned how little time she had left. The voices, whose messages had lately seemed confused to her, suddenly spoke out loud and clear. She later said:

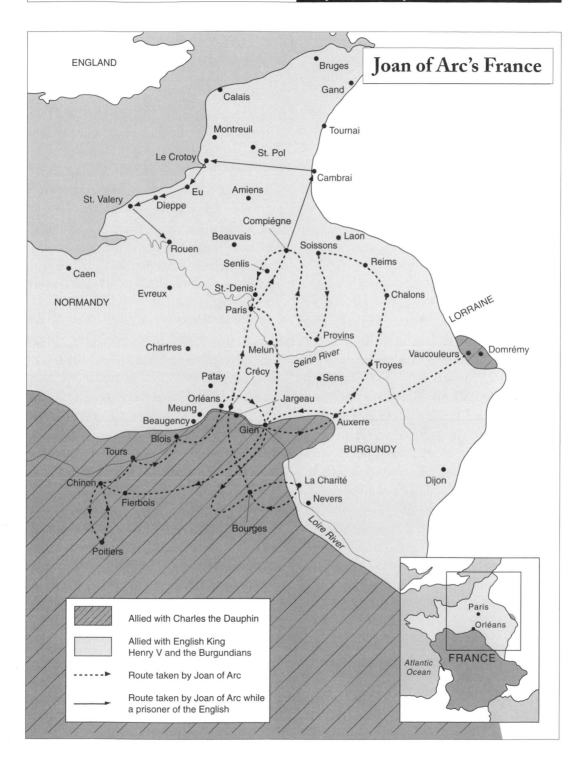

Joan of Arc's France

ENGLAND

Bruges
Gand
Calais
Montreuil
Tournai
St. Pol
Le Crotoy
Cambrai
Eu
Amiens
St. Valery
Dieppe
Compiégne
Beauvais
Laon
Rouen
Soissons
Senlis
Reims
Caen
St.-Denis
Evreux
Paris
Chalons
NORMANDY
LORRAINE
Chartres
Melun
Provins
Vaucouleurs
Domrémy
Crécy
Seine River
Troyes
Patay
Sens
Orléans
Jargeau
Meung
Beaugency
Auxerre
Blois
Gien
BURGUNDY
Tours
La Charité
Dijon
Chinon
Nevers
Fierbois
Bourges
Loire River
Poitiers

Allied with Charles the Dauphin

Allied with English King
Henry V and the Burgundians

- - - ▶ Route taken by Joan of Arc

───▶ Route taken by Joan of Arc while
a prisoner of the English

Paris
Orléans
Atlantic
Ocean
FRANCE

As I was on the ramparts of Melun, St. Catherine and St. Margaret warned me that I should be captured before Midsummer Day; that so it must needs be; nor must I be afraid and astounded; but take all things well, for God would help me. So they spoke, almost every day. And I prayed that when I was taken I might die in that hour, without wretchedness of long captivity; but the Voices said that so it must be.[34]

From Melun Joan moved on to Lagny, and there another miracle was attributed to her. In the church there she found the women of the town gathered around a baby in front of a statue of the Virgin. They told her the child had died three days earlier, before it could be baptized. When Joan looked, she saw that its body had turned black. Now Joan joined in the prayers for the child and when she did, color returned to its skin and it appeared to come to life and yawned three times. It was baptized immediately. Shortly afterward the baby died. It was buried in holy ground, and the townspeople praised Joan for saving its soul by bringing it back to life long enough to be baptized.

Compiègne

As the time allotted Joan by her voices dwindled, she became more determined to drive the enemy from Paris.

First, however, it was decided to secure the towns surrounding the capital city so the enemy would not have safe havens to flee to. On the road to Paris from the north stood Compiègne, a strongly fortified town at the confluence of the Aisne and Oise rivers. In making his foolish truce with the Duke of Burgundy, Charles had agreed to hand Compiègne over to him. The citizens of the town, however, had other ideas. They refused to hand the town over to the Duke of Burgundy and double-barred their gates against him.

The angry duke declared he would take the stubborn city by force. First he planned to take Choisy, a fortress just north of Compiègne that was held by forces loyal to the king. On May 13 Joan entered Compiègne from the south and received a warm welcome. The next day she and her troops attempted to capture the bridge that the Burgundians had to cross to reach Choisy. They had almost succeeded when enemy reinforcements arrived and drove them back. Two days later Choisy surrendered to the duke.

The only way now for Joan to cross the Aisne was by the bridge at the town of Soissons, some twenty-five miles down the river. She set out immediately, hoping to cross the river and surprise the Burgundians at Choisy by coming at them from behind. But the duke had been ahead

Burgundian Treachery

As 1430 began, Philip, the Duke of Burgundy, was at the height of his powers. In January his marriage to Princess Isabel of Portugal was celebrated with elaborate festivities. It was on this occasion that he founded the famous Order of the Golden Fleece,

setting himself up as a second King Arthur. He repeatedly postponed the promised peace conference with his cousin Charles VII until even the gullible Charles had to admit he had been deceived into signing meaningless truces and making unwarranted concessions to the Burgundian duke. Joan never for a minute trusted the good faith of the Burgundians or their English allies and repeatedly told the French king that he would find no peace except at the point of a lance.

By 1430 Philip, the Duke of Burgundy, was one of the most powerful men in western Europe.

of her and persuaded the governor of Soissons to refuse to allow her to pass. At this setback, most of the men Joan had been leading deserted the French army. Out of 1,500 men she was left with about 250. Greatly disappointed, Joan decided to return to Compiègne with her faithful few.

There she learned that the Burgundians had established several outposts close to the city walls in an attempt to surround Compiègne as they had surrounded Orléans when they besieged that town. Together with Guillaume de Flavy, the commander of the city, she planned a surprise attack on one of these outposts near the hamlet of Margny. Georges Chastellain, a contemporary historian who was not present but who gathered firsthand accounts of the events, described her as she prepared to set out on this mission:

She mounted her horse armed as would a man, adorned with a doublet of rich cloth-of-gold over her breastplate; she rode a very handsome, very proud gray courser and displayed herself in her armor and her bearing as a captain would have done . . . and in that array, with her standard raised high and fluttering in the wind, and well-accompanied by many noble men, she sallied forth from the city, about four hours past midday.[35]

Capture

With the men Flavy was able to supply, Joan had a total force of about five hundred for the sortie. As they rode out from Compiègne over the drawbridge on the Oise River, archers lined up on the ramparts to cover their retreat should that be needed. There were also boats on the river to pick up stragglers and keep them from being cut off. It was only a minor mission to demolish an outpost—no serious trouble was expected—and at first things went well for the French. The Burgundian garrison was not prepared for an attack. It seemed as though Joan and her soldiers would be able to destroy the outpost and withdraw to Compiègne without incident.

Unfortunately for the French, the Duke of Burgundy's second in com-

Reactions to Joan's Capture

In Joan of Arc *Regine Pernoud records descriptions of the moods of both camps as written by a Burgundian soldier who took part in the battle at Compiègne:*

> The French entered into Compiègne, doleful and wroth at their losses, and above all had great displeasure at the taking of the Maid. And on the contrary, they of the Burgundian side and the English were very joyous at it, more than had they taken five hundred combatants, for they feared and redoubted no other captain or chief in war as much as they had always done, until that day, this Maid.
>
> Quite soon after came the Duke of Burgundy with his power (forces) to his camp of Coudun where he was camped in a meadow before Compiègne, and there gathered the English, the Duke and those of the other camps, in very great number, making together great outcry and jollity for the taking of the Maid.

Burgundian soldiers capture Joan of Arc in 1430 as she attempts to retreat across a drawbridge into the city of Compiègne.

mand, John of Luxembourg, had chosen this time to make an inspection tour of the outposts near Compiègne. John was accompanied by his staff, but when he realized what was happening, he quickly sent for reinforcements from nearby outposts. Joan led the French in three attacks, but they were soon outnumbered as the troops John of Luxembourg had requested began arriv-

ing. As Joan's troops were forced back toward the town, she tried desperately to rally her soldiers. But the orderly retreat became a panicked flight as the French soldiers raced for the bridge, trying to beat the Burgundian soldiers who were trying to cut them off.

The opposing forces reached the bridge at the same time, and the archers on the wall could not cover the retreat for fear of killing their own men. Nevertheless most of the French soldiers managed to make their way over the bridge and through the gate into the safety of the town with the enemy on their heels. Seeing the mass of enemy soldiers approaching the city, Flavy ordered the drawbridge raised and the gate closed. Joan and a handful of her supporters, since they had been the last to retreat, were left outside. Immediately English and Burgundian fighting men swarmed around the little group. Recognizing the Maid, they called to her to yield.

Trapped but still fighting, Joan refused to yield until an enemy soldier seized her gold and scarlet surcoat and dragged her from her horse. She was taken into custody by the Duke of Luxembourg. It was the evening of May 23, 1430. The Maid of Orléans had fought her last battle.

Imprisonment

The English and their Burgundian allies and their French sympathizers were wild with joy at their good fortune. While Joan was still in Luxembourg's

Was Flavy a Traitor?

Historians still debate whether or not Guillaume de Flavy deliberately betrayed Joan on May 23, 1430. Did Flavy order the drawbridge raised with the intention of shutting her out from Compiègne so she could be captured? In 1934 J.B. Mestre published a book titled *Guillaume de Flavy Did Not Betray Joan of Arc*, in which he argues that Flavy was only trying to save his city. Other writers have reached different conclusions.

In *Joan of Arc: Her Story* authors Regine Pernoud and Marie Veronique Clin argue: "Careful study of the defense of Compiègne shows that there was no danger to the city even if the first gate of the palisade remained open so that Joan of Arc might have gained refuge. In the worst of cases, even if that gate had been taken, the city's defenses would have remained secure."

In *St. Joan of Arc* John Beevers concludes: "De Flavy, the governor of Compiègne, was either a fool or a coward, possibly both. To raise his drawbridge and leave the stragglers stranded, particularly when Joan was one of them, was a piece of appalling misjudgment. The right, natural, and easy thing to do was to lead forth a body of troops the moment he saw Joan's party in difficulties. He could comfortably have routed the English and the Burgundians and ensured that Joan reached safety."

Unless further evidence is uncovered, we can never know the truth about Flavy's motives.

camp, the Duke of Burgundy arrived to have a look at this young girl who had caused him so much grief. There is no record of what passed between them, but shortly afterward the duke wrote letters to the "good cities" of his realm boasting that the troublesome Pucelle was now a prisoner. "The fame of this capture shall spread throughout the world," he exulted, "and the news of it will expose the error and foolish beliefs of those who looked favorably upon the activities of this woman."[36]

Frenchmen who were loyal to the crown were deeply shocked and grieved by the news of Joan's capture. Prayers were offered for her deliverance and masses said for her in churches throughout the country. The king was besieged with letters begging him to use every means to regain her freedom, but as was his custom, Charles VII consulted his advisers. Unhappily for Joan, many of them were pleased to have a powerful rival like her removed from the scene.

What to do with the captive Maid was the burning question. The situation was complicated. By the laws of warfare of that time, Joan was the personal prisoner of John of Luxembourg, whose vassal had captured her. In turn John of Luxembourg was the vassal of the Duke of Burgundy, who in turn was the vassal of the king of England. From the time Joan had defeated them at Orléans, the English had called her a witch and threatened to capture and burn her. First, though, they would need to have her convicted by the church; otherwise they would have to treat her like any other high-ranking prisoner of war— eligible to be exchanged or ransomed.

For the five months that Luxembourg had charge of Joan, she was not treated unkindly. During her confinement at the fortress of Beaulieu, about twenty miles from Compiègne, she had as companions her steward d'Aulon and her brother Pierre. When she learned that she was to be transferred to a more distant site and separated from them, she made her first attempt to escape. Somehow she managed to shut her guard in the tower and had almost gotten away when the porter of the gate saw her and blocked her path.

During the summer of 1430 Joan was transferred to the castle of Beaurevoir, some thirty-seven miles from the fortress of Beaulieu. Here at the family seat of the Luxembourgs she was put into the care of three women: John of Luxembourg's wife, his aged aunt, and his stepdaughter. These women treated Joan with kindness and even affection. They tried to persuade John not to turn her over to the English. They also did their best to persuade her to abandon her masculine clothes, tempting her by offering her a choice of material from which her clothes could be made. Although Joan returned their kindly feelings, she refused to put on feminine clothing. Later she said that this was because God would not permit her to change the manner of her dress.

The English wished to gain custody over the imprisoned Joan and turn her over to the church to try her as a heretic.

The Miraculous Leap

While Joan was in the compassionate care of the Luxembourg ladies, intense negotiations were going on over who should be in charge of holding her. The English were demanding that John of Luxembourg turn her over to them immediately so they could have the church try her as a heretic.

The high churchman most eager in pressing for this disposition of the prized captive was Pierre Cauchon, bishop of Beauvais, who also was a close friend of the Duke of Burgundy. During the year of Joan's campaign to free France, Cauchon had had two humiliating experiences. First, he was forced to flee from Reims when the coronation took place there, and then he had been ousted from Beauvais when that town welcomed the Dauphin. Cauchon was afraid that Charles VII would ransom Joan before she could be brought to trial. He could not believe the French king would not try to rescue the girl who had set him on his throne.

Joan had often said she would rather die than fall into the hands of the English from whom she expected no mercy. She was also distressed by rumors that Compiègne was about to be captured and that the English had vowed to slaughter all the people over the age of seven when it fell. She thought that if only she could lead another attempt to free the town, she could succeed.

In her agony and despair she decided to jump from the castle tower in a desperate attempt to escape—or to commit suicide. The voice of St. Catherine warned her not to jump, but Joan for once defied her heavenly adviser. The distance from the roof of the tower to the ground was between sixty and seventy feet. When her astonished jailers discovered Joan, she was lying unconscious at the foot of the tower. Against all odds, she had broken no bones. She said of her recovery:

> After I fell from the tower, I was for two or three days without desire to eat, and I was so wounded in that jump that I could neither eat nor drink; but nevertheless, I had comfort from St. Catherine, who told me to confess myself and ask pardon from God for having jumped and that without fail the people of Compiègne would have help before the feast of St. Martin in the winter. And so I began to return to health; I began to eat and soon I was healed.[37]

Compiègne did indeed regain its freedom before the feast of St. Martin (November 11), but Joan would not be as fortunate. By then her circumstances would be much worse.

Chapter Seven

TRIAL AND CONDEMNATION

Joan had no one to defend her at her trial. She was supported only by her quick wits, her indomitable courage, and her unshakable belief that in everything she had done she was carrying out the will of God. Joan's persecutors were determined to condemn her in a way that would not make her a martyr, but they failed.

The Road to Rouen

It took some time to reach an agreement on who should have custody of Joan, but in November John of Luxembourg handed her over to the English in return for a payment of ten thousand gold crowns. It is difficult to equate that amount to modern currency, but historian Will Durant suggests it would have been the equivalent of about $250,000, a huge sum for that

day. Joan's worst fears were realized. She knew she could expect no mercy from the English, and she soon understood that she could expect no mercy from her church persecutors either.

Immediately after Joan was captured, Cauchon, who had strong connections to the University of Paris, had officials there write to the Duke of Burgundy and to John of Luxembourg asking that she be turned over to church officials to be tried for heresy. In a series of letters these officials requested that the church try her "because she is suspected and defamed to have committed many crimes, sortileges [enchantments], idolatry, invocations of enemies (devils) and other several cases touching our faith and against that faith."[38] They also requested that her trial be held in Paris.

The English were eager for the church to do the dirty work of condemning Joan, since that would justify condemning her to death. But they were not willing for her trial to take place in Paris. The capital was in a part of France that supported Charles VII, and the emotional climate would be strongly in her favor. Rouen, in northern France, was more favorable to the English. The city had been securely in English hands for more than a dozen years, and the surrounding country had been under English domination for so long that the people there seemed more English than French.

And so it was that Joan set off on what would be her last journey—from Beaurevoir to Rouen—in late November 1430. The trip took about a month, with stopovers in various towns. At Arras her Burgundian captors turned her over to an English escort of some fifty armed soldiers. Along the way people flocked to see the famous prisoner. At the castle of Drugy, near Saint-Riquier, she was visited by monks from the local abbey and by prominent citizens of the town. At Crotoy a boatload of women from Abbeville floated down the Somme River to visit her. They may have come out of curiosity, but they left with tears in their eyes. Joan was so impressed by the sympathy of the people in this area that she said, "What nice people they are! I should be very happy—when I come to die—if I could be buried among them."[39]

The Selling of Joan

John of Luxembourg, who held Joan captive, came of a noble house, but he was not a wealthy man. As the younger son of a younger son he could not count on much in the way of inheritance. According to the customs of the time, prisoners could be ransomed and set free, exchanged for prisoners of equal rank, or sold for hard cash. If Luxembourg expected the French king to offer a large ransom for his rich prize, he was soon disillusioned. The question of prisoner exchange was unrealistic; the French held no prisoners equal in value to the Maid. That left the option of selling her for the highest price possible. Luxembourg's aunt, who had grown fond of Joan while she was in her charge, begged him not to dishonor himself by selling her. His aunt's pleas may have restrained him temporarily, but when she died in September, he opened negotiations for the sale of his precious treasure.

A clergyman and scribe visit Joan of Arc in prison. During her transfer from Beaurevoir to Rouen, people flocked to visit the famous prisoner.

Two days before Christmas, Joan and her captors arrived in Rouen. Joan was placed in a dark cell in one of the towers of Rouen's castle. A few slits in the thick wall provided the only air and light. The room was dirty and bitterly cold. Because of her previous escape attempts, she was kept in irons both day and night. Her five guards were chosen from the most common soldiers; they constantly mocked and taunted her and threatened to rape her.

The Trial Begins

As onerous as her circumstances in jail was the torment of the trial itself. Pierre Cauchon, bishop of Beauvais, was the presiding judge. In addition to being a learned churchman, he was a clever politician. He hoped and expected that the English would make him archbishop of Rouen—after he tried and convicted Joan and made an example of her. With that in mind, he worked hard to gather an imposing tribunal. During the time the trial lasted, over four and a half months, the number of bishops, priests, doctors of theology, physicians, judges, and lawyers involved amounted to more than eighty.

On January 9, 1431, the court hearings began. The first phase of the trial lasted for six weeks, during which time the members considered the evidence against Joan and drew up the charges to be brought against her. They sent a committee to Domremy to gather facts about her life there. In her hometown the committee members heard nothing but good about her character as a young girl. They did, however, bring back stories about the Fairies' Tree and the fact that she had left home without her parents' permission.

From other sources, the judges collected stories to help prove charges of witchcraft and heresy: She foretold events before they happened; she boasted of what she would do in battle and then did it; she brought a dead child to life; she carried a banner that seemed to have magical powers; she tried to commit suicide; she obeyed voices that might be from the devil; and she disobeyed biblical teaching by wearing men's clothing. The few judges who protested that her actions were being twisted and that evidence in her favor was being ignored soon found themselves dismissed.

In the meantime, Joan remained in her cell, suffering physically and mentally. Since she was an ecclesiastical prisoner, she pleaded to be taken to a church prison, where her caretakers would be women. Instead she remained in iron shackles in the care of coarse soldiers who made her life miserable. She was denied all spiritual comforts of the church, and she had no privacy in which to commune with her voices.

There was a constant stream of unwelcome visitors. Many were curiosity seekers who simply came to see a suspected witch. Others came to question her in order to gather information that could be used against her by the court. Women were sent to examine her to see if she was a virgin as she claimed. They reported that she was.

The most dangerous visitors were spies sent by the court to worm their way into her confidence. The most damaging of these was Nicolas Loiseleur, a priest who pretended to be a fellow prisoner and who told her that he came from her native district of Lorraine. After he won her confidence, he offered to hear her confession. As always, Joan was more than willing to confess to a priest. What she did not know was that while she was talking or confessing to Loiseleur, two other men hid outside her cell writing down everything she said.

First Public Session

At last Pierre Cauchon was ready to begin the public trial. On Ash Wednesday, February 21, 1431, at about eight in the morning, Joan faced forty-four inquisitors, including nine doctors of theology, four doctors of church law, seven bachelors of theology, eleven licentiates (licensed practitioners) in canon law, and four in civil law in addition to Pierre Cauchon himself. Although prisoners accused of heresy usually were provided with a lawyer to defend them, Joan was denied this aid.

The judges quickly learned that months of confinement under harsh conditions had not crushed Joan's spirit. The first battle came with the opening formality, when Joan was asked to swear an oath to tell the truth. Bishop

The Mock Trial

Since the English rulers were determined that Joan should die, why did they not simply execute her? The answer is that it was important to them that she be tried and found guilty and publicly discredited as a heretic inspired by the devil. Although they turned her over to the French church authorities to be tried, they made it clear that they would determine her fate if the outcome of the trial did not please them. In *St. Joan of Arc* John Beevers quotes from a letter written by the English regents acting for the nine-year-old English king. In it they state that they are delivering Joan to Cauchon, the French bishop of Beauvais "so that he may examine and question her and proceed against her according to God, the divine law, and the holy canons." After listing various crimes she had allegedly committed, the letter ends with the warning: "Nevertheless, we intend to seize and regain possession of this Joan if it should happen that she is not convicted or found guilty of the said crimes."

Although prisoners in heresy trials were entitled to legal representation, Joan was forced to stand trial alone in 1431.

Cauchon urged her: "Swear to tell the truth concerning whatever will be asked you that has to do with the Catholic faith and with anything else that you know," and she replied: "About my father and mother, and everything that I have done since I took the road to come to France, I shall willingly swear; but never have I said or revealed anything about the revelations made to me by God except to Charles, my king. And even if you wish to cut my head off, I will not reveal them, because I know from my visions that I must keep them secret."[40] Cauchon repeatedly exhorted her to take the oath, and she repeatedly refused to take it on the terms the bishop imposed. At last she knelt and placed her hand on the book of the Gospels and swore to answer truthfully any questions on matters of faith. With that limited oath her inquisitors had to be content.

As the questioning proceeded, the tribunal soon ran into other obstacles. When Cauchon asked Joan to say the paternoster (Lord's Prayer), she responded that she would only say it to him in confession. Then he told her that if she tried to escape, she would be automatically convicted of heresy. But she refused to accept that idea, saying she had not taken an oath not to try to escape, claiming that prisoners have the right to attempt to regain their freedom.

There were six public sessions, during which the examiners probed Joan's entire life. During the long, exhausting sessions, questions were not asked in an orderly fashion but came at Joan from all directions so that she often asked the judges to wait their turns. Often the questions were tricky or repetitious with the intent of catching her in a contradiction. Joan refused to be intimidated. She did not hesitate to tell them to "Pass on," when she felt she had already given a sufficient answer to a question. She even had the audacity to warn her judges that they were themselves in danger of incurring God's wrath: "Take care of what you say, for, as my judges, you are assuming a terrible responsibility."[41]

Over and over again she was questioned about the voices that she had said directed her actions and about her refusal to wear women's clothing. She would put on women's clothing if they permitted her to go to Mass, she said, and if afterward she could go free. She further said that her voices were still directing her, advising her to speak out bravely in the courtroom.

When she told them, "If it were not for the grace of God, I would not know how to do anything," an interrogator suddenly asked, "Do you know if you are in the grace of God?" It was a dangerous question, and a presumptuous answer might establish her as a heretic. One of the clerics told her she need not respond to it, but her simple, eloquent answer stunned the courtroom. She replied: "If I am not, may God put me there. And if I am, may God keep me there, for I would be the most sorrowful woman in the world if I knew that I was not in the grace of God."[42]

The public sessions, which ended on March 3, were a failure in that nothing had been proven against Joan. In fact, her direct, truthful answers had impressed a number of the judges, and they refused to take further part in what they realized was a farcical trial. Cauchon, however, was determined to press forward. Accordingly, from March 10 to March 17, he and a select few like-minded judges visited Joan in her cell in order to continue to try to make her convict herself by her own testimony.

The Articles of Accusation

During these closed sessions, questions about her clothing and about the voices that guided her conduct were continually raised. The purpose behind the questions was clearly to prove that Joan was unwilling to submit to the church's authority and was therefore a heretic. Joan continued to answer with spirit. She would gladly submit to the will of the church, she said, *after* she had

Charles's Inertia

The only remote reference we have to any action Charles VII might have taken to save Joan is in a journal kept by a merchant named Antonio Morosini. He notes a

rumor that the French king has threatened the Burgundians with retaliation if they sell Joan to the English. There is no documentary evidence that the king tried to ransom Joan or to rescue her by negotiation or by military force. In all the months Joan spent in captivity she received not a word from Charles. The remarkable thing is that instead of resenting his abandonment, she refused to hear a bad word said about him and died believing him worthy of her praise and devotion.

There is no historical evidence to suggest King Charles VII attempted to have Joan rescued.

obeyed the will of God as revealed to her through her visions and voices. Several times she asked to be taken to the pope so he could judge whether or not she was guilty of heresy, but these requests were ignored.

The closed-door investigation ended on March 18, and a week later the public trial resumed. As ordered by the judges, the court clerk had drawn up an Act of Accusation against Joan. It contained seventy separate charges, which were read to her over a period of three days. The charges summed up the rumors, misstatements, half-truths, and outright lies about her behavior that had been brought out during the questioning periods. They concluded: "The said accused . . . has performed, composed and commanded many charms and superstitions; she has been deified and has permitted herself to be adored and venerated; she has called up demons and evil spirits, has consulted and frequented them."[43] Joan denied each of the charges as it was read.

While in prison, Joan became seriously ill as a result of the strain and the conditions of prison life.

Following the reading of the Act of Accusation, a committee set to work to reduce the list to twelve concise accusations to be used as a basis for the rest of the trial. In the meantime, Joan became seriously ill, a consequence of the strain she was under and the conditions in which she was forced to live. Afraid that she might die before they could convict her, the inquisitors summoned the best doctors available to treat her, and she recovered.

The Trial Ends

On April 18, while Joan was still feverish and confined to her bed, the next phase of the trial began. In the language of the church authorities, this was called the "Charitable Warnings." Cauchon and several other churchmen visited Joan and pleaded with her to confess her sins (as outlined in the twelve articles) and submit to the authority of the church. If she did so, they promised she would be allowed to receive the sacraments of the church. Wearily she repeated what she had so often told them: She loved the church, but first and always she would obey God's commands even if it meant she would lose her life. At the second charitable warning or admonition session on May 2, she appeared before sixty members of the court, repeated the same litany, and again asked to be taken to the pope. Again her request was refused.

Frustrated by this stubborn young woman who would not admit that she was wrong, her judges set out to wear Joan down. On May 9 she was taken to the torture chamber of the castle, where Cauchon warned her that if she did not tell the truth, she would be tortured until she confessed. Joan looked around the room at the rack, the knives, the spikes, the pincers, the glowing coals, and the two hefty men waiting to apply them and answered calmly: "Truly, though you were to have my limbs torn off and send the soul out of my body, I should not say otherwise; and if I did tell you otherwise, I should always thereafter say that you made me speak by force."[44] After some behind-the-scenes consultations, the judges decided that physical torture would not serve their purpose.

On May 23, 1431, exactly one year after her capture at Compiègne, Joan's trial formally concluded. She was led to a room in the castle to appear before Cauchon and ten other church dignitaries. The indictment against her was read, and she was admonished to recant (retract) her testimony and submit to the judgment of the church. Despite the months of spiritual torment and her physical weakness, she replied defiantly: "If at this moment I saw the stake, the faggots [wood fuel], the executioner lighting the fire, and if I stood in the middle of it, I would not say anything else, and I would say until death only what I said at the trial."[45] At that time she had exactly one week of life left.

Chapter Eight

FIRE AND REDEMPTION

Joan's martyrdom began on May 30, 1431, when she was burned at the stake in the Old Market Square in Rouen. Her redemption began twenty-five years later when a trial of rehabilitation was held, and she was declared innocent of all charges brought by the first trial.

At the Cemetery of Saint-Ouen

On May 24 the church officials made a final effort to wring from Joan a confession that would justify her conviction as a heretic. In the spacious cemetery of the Abbey of Saint-Ouen, one of the great churches of Rouen, they set up a scene designed to shake her resolve.

Several platforms were erected. On one stand sat Pierre Cauchon, bishop of Beauvais, representing the church in France, and Henry Beaufort, bishop of Winchester, representing the church in England. Below them were arranged other bishops, abbots, priors, and lesser clergymen. Joan was led through a large crowd of English soldiers and citizens of the town to a smaller platform, where she was seated on a wooden stool. To one side she could see the red-clad executioner and his assistants waiting.

Exhausted from months of relentless questioning, alone and friendless, she sat with her head bowed as a sermon was preached to her. The preacher was Master Guillaume Erard, a friend of Cauchon and of the English. He took as his text the words Jesus spoke to his disciples as recorded in John 15: 2–4: "Every branch in me that beareth not fruit he taketh away . . . the branch cannot bear fruit of itself, except it abide in the vine." Then, declaring that

France had never known such a monster as Joan, he called her a witch, a magician, and a heretic.

Joan sat immobile listening to the familiar accusations—until Erard included the king in his charges: "Charles who calls himself King has adhered like a heretic and schismatic [dissenter] to the words of a woman vain and defamed and of all dishonour full." Pointing at Joan, he said, "It is to thee, Joan, that I speak, and I tell thee that thy King is a heretic and schismatic." At these words Joan suddenly came to life, crying out: "By my faith, sir, with respect, I dare to tell you and swear to you on pain of my life that he is the noblest Christian of all the Christians."[46]

What happened next is still being debated. Written records confirm that following the sermon, Joan was exhorted three times to submit to the church and admit she had not obeyed its teachings. Her request to appeal to the pope was again denied. Then Cauchon began reading the sentence by which she would be turned over to the civil authorities, who would give her to the executioners waiting to take her to the stake to be burned.

As the sentence was being read, priests clamored for her to recant and some people in the crowd began throwing stones toward the stand. A document of abjuration (retraction) was produced. The historian Edward Wagenknecht says:

Before sentencing Joan, church officials made one final attempt to wrest from her a confession of heresy.

What happened is even yet none too clear. She may have been tricked by having one paper read to her and another substituted for it. She may have been simply frightened out of her wits. Or she may have been mentally tortured into such a condition of irresponsibility that she had no idea what she was doing. . . . This was her only moment of spiritual surrender.[47]

Whatever actually happened, her judges believed she had at last agreed

Joan signs the document of abjuration, submitting to the judgment of the tribunal. Historians continue to debate her motive for doing so.

to submit to the judgment of the tribunal, and Cauchon pronounced a sentence of life imprisonment.

The Last Days

Joan expected that she would be taken to a church prison where she would have women to care for her, but again this turned out not to be the case. Cauchon ordered the guards to take her back to the same cell where the English soldiers were waiting to taunt her. One condition in her recantation was that she was to resume dressing as a woman. She complied, but in a matter of days the soldiers hid her woman's clothing, and in order to be clothed, she was forced to put on her man's doublet and hose which had been left in her cell.

When Cauchon learned she had resumed male attire, he hurried to the prison accompanied by several other judges. She told them she would rather die than remain in irons, and begged that, as had been promised, she should be taken to a church prison and placed under the care of women.

When the judges asked her if she had heard the voices of saints Margaret and Catherine since the recantation ceremony, she replied that she had. Joan went on, "My voices have since told me that I did a great injury in confessing that I had not done well in what I had done. All that I said and revoked that Thursday, I did only because of fear of the fire." The clerk who was making a written record of the meeting wrote in the margin of his page "fatal answer."[48]

In the eyes of the church Joan was now a relapsed heretic. Cauchon hastily convened forty-two principal judges together to assess her behavior. They agreed she had relapsed and should be handed over to the secular authorities for punishment. The following morning, May 30, two monks arrived at her

Joan's Prison

In Joan of Arc: Her Story *authors Regine Pernoud and Marie Veronique Clin describe the procedural trickery used to keep Joan imprisoned under the harsh conditions to which she was subjected:*

Pierre Cauchon and the University of Paris intended to try her for heresy, so this had to be a church trial. According to normal canon-law procedure, Joan should have been detained in an ecclesiastical prison, guarded by women; and thus she would have received moderately humane treatment. Yet throughout the trial Joan was treated as a prisoner of war, chained and guarded by soldiers. To disguise this legal inconsistency, the bishop of Beauvais [Cauchon] and the Duke of Bedford had recourse to a legal fiction: The lock of the door of her prison cell was secured by three keys, of which one was to be kept by Cardinal Henry Beaufort, bishop of Winchester, who was to be present during the trial's entirety, and the two others to be held by judges. . . . Since all three were clerics, the fiction could be maintained that she was entirely subject to ecclesiastical custody.

cell to hear her confession and give her Communion. She lamented to them: "Oh! That I should be treated so cruelly! That my pure and unblemished body, which has never been defiled, must today be burned to ashes! I'd rather have my head cut off seven times than be burned like this." And when Cauchon entered her cell, she exclaimed, "My Lord Bishop, I die because of you."[49]

The Stake

Following the final confrontation with Cauchon, Joan left her cell for the last time, dressed in a long white robe. She was placed in a cart to be taken to the Old Market Square of Rouen. Enormous crowds lined the streets to stare at the girl who had led French troops to triumph over English armies and brought the king to his crowning at Reims.

The marketplace was jammed with citizens and a thousand English soldiers. Joan was led to a platform where she stood for nearly an hour while a sermon was preached. She listened quietly until the priest ended by saying, "Jeanne, go in peace, the Church can no longer protect you, and delivers you into secular hands."[50] At that she knelt and prayed in a trembling voice to God to forgive those who had wronged her and begged those who were present to pray for her soul. Some of the high churchmen who had condemned her also wept, and some were so overcome they had to leave the marketplace.

When she asked for a crucifix, an English soldier, moved by pity, quickly made a little cross out of two pieces of wood and gave it to a monk to hand to her. Kissing the cross, she placed it in the bosom of her white dress. Then she asked that a large crucifix be brought from the nearby church. It was nearly noontime, and the English soldiers were growing impatient for their dinner. Rough hands seized her and she was pushed toward the scaffold where the stake and the bundles of sticks were waiting. A tall paper cap was placed on her head. On it were written the words "Heretic, Relapsed, Apostate, Idolatress." As she was bound to the stake, she told the monk holding the large crucifix to get down from the scaffolding to safety, but she asked him to continue to hold the crucifix so she could see it.

The executioner lit the sticks around her feet. While the flames crackled and rose, she repeatedly called out the name of Jesus. As the fire enveloped her, her head bowed forward and her voice stopped. Her anguish was over. One English official expressed his opinion that a grave error had been made. As he watched the flames destroy her, John Tressart, secretary to the king of England, exclaimed, "We are lost; we have burnt a saint."[51]

When her body had burned to ashes, the executioner obeyed orders to throw them into the river Seine. Joan's persecutors had not wanted her

Joan of Arc prays to God as she is burned at the stake in Rouen. As the flames engulfed her, she repeatedly called out the name of Jesus.

Joan's Family

Joan's father Jacques d'Arc died in 1431. It was said that he died of sorrow over his daughter's tragic end. After the Trial of Rehabilitation and the celebrations following the declaration of Joan's innocence, her mother Isabelle lived for two years, dying in November of 1458. Joan's brother Jean became governor of Vaucouleurs. Her brother Pierre, who had been captured with Joan at Compiègne, died soon after their mother. Although both brothers had children, their descendants have disappeared from history.

remains to be buried, since they knew her grave would become a shrine and her memory the fuel of continued resistance to English rule. They soon discovered, however, that it was easier to destroy her body than it was to extinguish memory of her.

At first, for about a year after Joan's death, the English cause in France seemed strong. They won several military victories, and the boy-king Henry VI was crowned king of France at Paris on December 16, 1431. However, the city of Reims refused to let him be consecrated with the holy oil kept there, and most Frenchmen considered the ceremony meaningless. Cauchon took part in the coronation, but the English, realizing that he was hated and despised by large numbers of Frenchmen, did not award him the position of archbishop of Rouen for which he had hoped.

Over the next few years French forces began to gain the upper hand over the English. When the regent Duke of Bedford died in 1435, an accord was reached between the Burgundians and the French. After this loss of their ally, the English were gradually pushed out of the country.

Rehabilitation

Twenty-two years passed after Joan's execution. Paris fell to the French. The French acquired a new light cannon that fired lead shot that easily destroyed lines of English archers. By 1453 the English had been driven out of France, and the Hundred Years' War was over.

Joan the Maid had not been forgotten. Poems were written about her, prayers were said for her, and her memory continued to inspire French soldiers as they went into battle. When the English withdrew from Rouen, Charles VII entered the city in triumph. One of his first acts in Rouen was to order Guillaume Bouille, former rector of the University of Paris, to begin an inquiry into Joan's trial.

Historians have long speculated on the king's motives in this matter. Although Charles had made no effort to save Joan, he may have wanted to clear her reputation simply because he felt she deserved it. However, many historians point out that Charles undoubtedly also stood to gain by removing the stain of having been put on his throne by a convicted heretic.

Bouille questioned a number of witnesses and reported his findings to Charles, who asked the church to authorize a new trial for Joan. Pope Calixtus III authorized Joan's remaining family (her aged mother and two brothers) to ask for rehabilitation for Joan. On November 17, 1455, the first session of the new trial opened in the cathedral of Notre Dame in Paris.

A host of supporters and well-wishers surrounded Joan's mother, Isabelle, as she tearfully voiced her plea to the judges. Telling them she had brought up her daughter to be "respectful and faithful" toward the church, Isabelle said: "Then, although she had not thought, or plotted or done anything not according to the faith . . . envious persons wishing her evil . . . embroiled her in an ecclesiastical trial . . . wickedly condemning her at the last and burning her."[52]

The tribunal moved from Paris to Rouen, with inquests held at Orléans and Domremy. In contrast to Joan's first trial, hosts of people were now allowed to testify in her behalf. Companions from her youth, old comrades-at-arms, members of the royal family such as the Duke of Alençon, all enthusiastically praised her character and her devotion to the church. A number of the judges from the original trial were called to testify concerning the improper procedures that took place at that time. Point by point Joan's testimony was considered and weighed.

Finally, on July 7, 1456, the court declared:

> The said trial and sentence (of condemnation) being tainted with fraud, calumny [perjury], iniquity, contradiction and manifest errors of fact and law, including the abjuration, execution, and all their consequences, to have been and to be null, invalid, worthless, without effect and annihilated. . . . We proclaim that Joan did not contract any taint of infamy and that she shall be and is washed clean of such.[53]

In May 1920, exactly 489 years after the flames consumed her body in the marketplace at Rouen, Joan was declared a saint by Pope Benedict XV. Saint Joan is the national heroine of France, but her veneration is not restricted to her native country. Her memory has been and continues to be worshipped by hundreds of thousands of people around the world. Scholars will likely never completely solve the mysteries of Joan of Arc's life: the voices

The Source of Joan's Power

In St. Joan of Arc Vita Sackville-West points out that Joan possessed no special qualifications for her tremendous mission, but she had something more important:

She did possess the power to accomplish what she had undertaken. Her courage and conviction were superhuman. They were of the quality which admits no doubt and recognises no obstacle. Her own absolute faith was the secret of her strength. This is not at all the same thing as claiming for her that she was a great military genius, as even that cautious and experienced commander Marshal Foch has claimed. Her good sense we may freely acknowledge, and her gift, which Foch pointed out, "of dealing with the situation as each new day presented it"; but if we are to claim genius for her at all, we must be more comprehensive and less specific: we must grant her the genius of personality. No easier to define than charm or beauty, in

Jeanne's case we can come somewhere near a definition by saying that this all-pervading forcefulness sprang from the intensity of her inner persuasions. This it is ... which raised her psychological value as a leader so far above her tactical or strategical value. It was her single-mindedness which enabled her to inspire disheartened men and to bend reluctant princes to her will.

Some historians believe Joan's courage and conviction made her such an effective military leader.

and visions, her prophecies, or the miracles she is said to have performed. There is no question, though, that she overcame incredible obstacles to become an inspiring symbol and to accomplish truly amazing feats. And her life continues to intrigue outstanding artists, sculptors, poets, playwrights, novelists, and biographers throughout the world. For many, the words of Mark Twain, one of her greatest admirers, hold true. He called her "by far the most extraordinary person the human race has ever produced."[54]

Notes

Chapter One: Life in Domremy

1. Quoted in Regine Pernoud, *Joan of Arc*, trans. Edward Hyams. New York: Stein and Day, 1982, p. 16.

2. Quoted in Pernoud, *Joan of Arc*, p. 17.

3. Quoted in Pernoud, *Joan of Arc*, pp. 19–20.

4. Will Durant, *The Story of Civilization*, vol. 6, *The Reformation*. New York: Simon and Schuster, 1957, p. 70.

5. Quoted in Vita Sackville-West, *Saint Joan of Arc*. New York: Doubleday, Doran, 1938, p. 56.

Chapter Two: The Mission Begins

6. Quoted in Regine Pernoud and Marie Veronique Clin, *Joan of Arc: Her Story*, trans. Jeremy du Quesnay Adams. New York: St. Martin's, 1999, p. 19.

7. Quoted in John Beevers, *St. Joan of Arc*. Rockford, IL: Tan, 1981, p. 43.

8. Quoted in Pernoud, *Joan of Arc*, pp. 39–40.

9. Quoted in Jay Williams, *Joan of Arc*.
New York: American Heritage, 1963, p. 35.

10. Beevers, *St. Joan of Arc*, p. 49.

Chapter Three: Orléans Is Delivered

11. Quoted in Pernoud and Clin, *Joan of Arc*, p. 34.

12. Quoted in Pernoud, *Joan of Arc*, p. 63.

13. Quoted in Beevers, *St. Joan of Arc*, pp. 61–62.

14. Quoted in Pernoud and Clin, *Joan of Arc*, pp. 39–40.

15. Quoted in Williams, *Joan of Arc*, p. 44.

16. Quoted in Pernoud and Clin, *Joan of Arc*, p. 42.

17. Quoted in Laura E. Richards, *Joan of Arc*. New York: Appleton, 1924, p. 125.

18. Quoted in Pernoud and Clin, *Joan of Arc*, p. 44.

Chapter Four: The Glorious Spring

19. Quoted in Pernoud and Clin, *Joan of Arc*, p. 57.

20. Quoted in Pernoud and Clin, *Joan of Arc*, p. 59.

21. Quoted in Pernoud and Clin, *Joan of Arc*, p. 60.

22. Quoted in Richards, *Joan of Arc*, p. 175.

23. Quoted in Pernoud, *Joan of Arc*, p. 123.

24. Quoted in Edward Wagenknecht, ed., *Joan of Arc: An Anthology of History and Literature*. New York: Creative Age, 1948, p. 10.

25. Quoted in Pernoud and Clin, *Joan of Arc*, p. 66.

Chapter Five: From Reims to Paris

26. Quoted in Williams, *Joan of Arc*, p. 86.

27. Quoted in Pernoud, *Joan of Arc*, p. 131.

28. Quoted in Williams, *Joan of Arc*, p. 91.

29. Quoted in Pernoud and Clin, *Joan of Arc*, p. 77.

30. Quoted in Williams, *Joan of Arc*, p. 98.

31. Quoted in Beevers, *St. Joan of Arc*, pp. 105–06.

32 Quoted in Pernoud and Clin, *Joan of Arc*, pp. 80–81.

33. Quoted in Pernoud and Clin, *Joan of Arc*, p. 81.

Chapter Six: Capture and Imprisonment

34. Quoted in Richards, *Joan of Arc*, p. 227.

35. Quoted in Pernoud and Clin, *Joan of Arc*, p. 86.

36. Quoted in Beevers, *St. Joan of Arc*, p. 112.

37. Quoted in Pernoud and Clin, *Joan of Arc*, p. 96.

Chapter Seven: Trial and Condemnation

38. Quoted in Pernoud, *Joan of Arc*, pp. 157–58.

39. Quoted in Beevers, *St. Joan of Arc*, p. 121.

40. Quoted in Pernoud and Clin, *Joan of Arc*, p. 109.

41. Quoted in Beevers, *St. Joan of Arc*, p. 131.

42. Quoted in Pernoud and Clin, *Joan of Arc*, pp. 111–12.

43. Quoted in Williams, *Joan of Arc*, p. 126.

44. Quoted in Pernoud, *Joan of Arc*, p. 206.

45. Quoted in Williams, *Joan of Arc*, p. 128.

Chapter Eight: Fire and Redemption

46. Quoted in Pernoud, *Joan of Arc*, p. 211.

47. Wagenknecht, *Joan of Arc*, p. 17.

48. Quoted in Pernoud, *Joan of Arc*, p. 221.

49. Quoted in Beevers, *St. Joan of Arc*, p. 169.

50. Quoted in Sackville-West, *Saint Joan of Arc*, p. 340.

51. Quoted in Sackville-West, *Saint Joan of Arc*, p. 342.

52. Quoted in Mary Gordon, *Joan of Arc*. New York: Penguin Putnam, 2000, p. 133.

53. Quoted in Pernoud, *Joan of Arc*, p. 269.

54. Mark Twain, *Joan of Arc*. San Francisco: Ignatius, 1899, p. 452.

For Further Reading

Books

Susan Banfield, *Joan of Arc.* Philadelphia: Chelsea House, 1987. The best feature of this biography is the military history.

Polly Schoyer Brooks, *Beyond the Myth: The Story of Joan of Arc.* Minneapolis, MN: Sagebrush Educational Resources, 1999. A scholarly biography, rich in details about Joan's life and the times in which she lived.

Mabel Dodge Holmes, *Joan of Arc: The Life Story of the Maid of Orleans.* Chicago: John C. Winston, 1930. Historical fiction that contains a helpful pronunciation guide to French names.

Elisabeth Kyle, *Maid of Orleans: The Story of Joan of Arc.* Edinburgh: Thomas Nelson, 1957. Historical fiction with an easy to read narrative style.

Jeannette Covert Nolan, *The Story of Joan of Arc.* New York: Grosset & Dunlap, 1953. Historical fiction that takes some liberties with history but is a pleasant retelling of Joan's story.

Josephine Poole, *Joan of Arc.* New York: Knopf Books for Young Readers, forthcoming August, 2005. Beautifully illustrated biography tells Joan's story in simple, evocative language. Maps and complete chronology.

Stephen W. Richey, *Joan of Arc: The Warrior Saint.* Westport, CT: Greenwood Publishing Group, 2003. Uses eyewitness accounts from Joan's military cohorts.

Nancy Wilson Ross, *Joan of Arc.* Minneapolis, MN: Sagebrush Education Resources, 2003. A straightforward, readable account of Joan's ability to accomplish her goals because of her deep belief that she was divinely inspired.

Diane Stanley, *Joan of Arc.* New York: Harper Trophy, 2002. This excellent biography tells the story of Joan and her times in clear and interesting detail. The illustrations, done in the style of illuminated manuscripts of the time, are impressive.

Video

Biography: Joan of Arc. A & E Entertainment, 1999. One of A&E's "Legendary Women" series. Lush photographs of historical scenes and images and thought provoking interviews with leading scholars.

The Messenger: The Story of Joan of Arc. Columbia Pictures, 2003. Milla Jovovich, John Malkovich, Faye Dunaway, and Dustin Hoffman star in this dramatic epic.

The Passion of Joan of Arc by Carl Dreyers. (Criterion Landmark Film) Originally a 1928 silent film, now a striking 21st century DVD restoration.

Internet Sources

Danuta Bois, 1999, contributor. (http://www.distinguishedwomen. com/biographies/joanarc.html).

Short, factual biography of Joan.

Saint Joan of Arc Center Albuquerque, N. M. (http://www.stjoan@stjoan-center.com). Extensive bibliography of materials available on Joan of arc.

Allen Williamson, Joan of Arc Online Archive. (http:members.aol.com/ hywwebsite/private/joanofarc.html). Nearly three hundred pages currently online. Includes biography, bibliography, letters, trial documents, portraits, timeline, and Web site links.

WORKS CONSULTED

C. Allmand, *Henry V*. Berkeley, CA: University of California Press, 1992. Joan of Arc from Shakespeare's perspective.

_____, *The Hundred Years' War: England and France at War*. Cambridge: Cambridge University Press, 1988. Good background material on politics in the time of Joan of Arc.

John Beevers, *St. Joan of Arc*. Rockford, IL: Tan, 1981. A readable, interpretative biography. Does not have notes, bibliography, or index.

Will Durant, *The Story of Civilization*. Vol. 6, *The Reformation*. New York: Simon and Schuster, 1957. Good background material on religion and politics in France and in Europe during the Middle Ages.

Mary Gordon, *Joan of Arc*. New York: Penguin Putnam, 2000. A lyrical retelling of Joan's story. Gordon explores the Maid's motivation and the mysteries surrounding her.

Wilfred T. Jewkes and Jerome B. Landfield, *Joan of Arc: Fact, Legend, and Literature*. New York: Harcourt, Brace & World, 1964. An anthology containing selections from the records of Joan's trial and retrial, selections from Holinshed's *Chronicles*, the official pronouncement of her canonization, and the plays written about her by Schiller, Shaw, and Anouilh.

Douglas Murray. *Jeanne d'Arc, Maid of Orleans*. (Heinemann, 1902) An English translation of the trial with an interesting introduction.

Regine Pernoud, *Joan of Arc*. Trans. Edward Hyams. New York: Stein and Day, 1982. Historical biography using letters, chronicles, and trial records to portray Joan as her contemporaries saw her.

Regine Pernoud and Marie Veronique Clin, *Joan of Arc: Her Story*. Trans. Jeremy duQuesnay Adams. New York: St. Martin's, 1999. This biography by two distinguished French women was a best seller in France. Adams has added an extremely useful glossary which includes portraits of the important people in Joan's world as well as synopses of historical occurrences of the times.

Laura E. Richards, *Joan of Arc*. New York: Appleton, 1924. The author has written a fictionalized biography that is readable and faithful to the facts of Joan's life.

Vita Sackville-West, *Saint Joan of Arc.* New York: Doubleday, Doran, 1938. An excellent biography with helpful footnotes, appendices, bibliography, and index.

Mark Twain, *Joan of Arc.* San Francisco: Ignatius, 1899. Mark Twain, who spent twelve years researching this fictionalized biography, considered it his best work. His deep admiration for Joan shows on every page.

Edward Wagenknecht, ed., *Joan of Arc: An Anthology of History and Literature.* New York: Creative Age, 1948. Wagenknecht presents a cross section of writings by more than thirty historians, biographers, essayists, philosophers, and poets on the subject of Joan of Arc. All aspects of her character and behavior are examined in fascinating and often contradictory detail.

Jay Williams, *Joan of Arc.* New York: American Heritage, 1963. One in a series of Horizon Caravel books by the editors of Horizon Magazine. Superb collection of illustrations includes paintings, manuscript miniatures, woodcuts, sculptures, photographs, and maps pertaining to Joan's life.

Periodicals

Susan Crane, "Clothing and Gender Definition: Joan of Arc," *Journal of Medieval and Early Modern Studies*, no. 2 (1996): 297-320.

INDEX